Y0-BVN-139

Present and Past

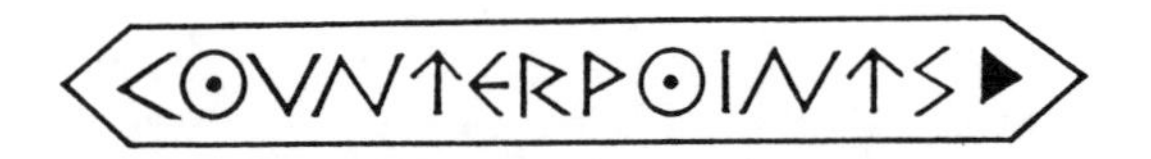

Studies in the Postmodern Theory of Education

Joe L. Kincheloe and Shirley R Steinberg
General Editors

Vol. 6

PETER LANG
New York • Washington, D.C./Baltimore • San Francisco
Bern • Frankfurt am Main • Berlin • Vienna • Paris

Clinton B. Allison

Present and Past

Essays for Teachers in the History of Education

PETER LANG
New York • Washington, D.C./Baltimore • San Francisco
Bern • Frankfurt am Main • Berlin • Vienna • Paris

Library of Congress Cataloging-in-Publication Data

Allison, Clinton B.
Present and past: essays for teachers in the history of education/ Clinton B. Allison.
p. cm—(Counterpoints; vol. 6)
Includes bibliographical references and index.
1. Public schools—United States—History. I. Title. II. Series: Counterpoints (New York, N.Y.); vol. 6.
LA212.A44 371'.01' 0973—dc20 94-40523
ISBN 0-8204-1780-7 (pbk.)
ISSN 1058-1634

Die Deutsche Bibliothek-CIP-Einheitsaufnahme

Allison, Clinton B.:
Present and Past: essays for teachers in the history of education/
Clinton B. Allison - New York; Washington D.C./Baltimore; San Francisco; Bern; Frankfurt am Main; Berlin; Vienna; Paris; Lang.
(Counterpoints; Vol. 6.)
ISBN 0-8204-1780-7
NE: GT

Illustration on the cover by Robert M. Cothran, Jr.

Cover design by Nona Reuter.

The paper in this book meets the guidelines for permanence and durability of the Committee on Production Guidelines for Book Longevity of the Council on Library Resources.

Printed in the United States of America.

For
Allison Constanza
Natalie Ann
Emma Gillian
Elena Claudia
and
Elijah Clinton Monroe

Contents

Foreword

Joe L. Kincheloe

The late twentieth century is an era beset by historical ignorance. Education is an institution that suffers from social amnesia. Together these two factors work to undermine educators' understanding of their historical location in the web of reality. As a result, American schooling operates under a mind-set of planned obsolescence where education, like American automobiles, avoids substantive change by creating the illusion that it is perpetually new. As the past is forgotten, it shapes the present without resistance. Everything that exists is natural; it could not have come to exist in any other form. Thus, school has taken the form the gods meant for it to take. Such historical unconsciousness does not free us from the past; on the contrary it captures us in the net of obliviousness.

Clinton Allison's book is not entitled *Present and Past* by accident. He believes, unlike some in his field, that the past cannot be separated from the present–indeed, the past can be understood only as it continues to live in the present. It is this connection between past and present that moves Allison's history. Though he may be guilty of many things, Allison is no necrophiliac–he approaches history with no need to fetishize or romanticize the dead. He knows that educational history lives, that it is central to our attempt to understand the workings of present-day social, psychological, and educational processes and their subtle interrelationships. Contrary to what the antiquarians, the necrophiliacs, might argue, educational historians will be judged by the contributions they make in putting their knowledge of the past to work in the attempt to understand pedagogy in the present and to shape its future. The point is so obvious that it might not be worth stressing except for the fact that many historians have worked so hard to deny it.

Explicit in his concern with connecting the past and present, Allison moves into the realm of memory—more specifically, dangerous educational memory. The word, memory, directs the attention of historians away from an exclusive concern with the past toward a concern with the past-present relationship. Memory unlike history has a verb form—to remember. Because the past lives in the present (certainly it lives in the minds of those who inhabit the present) memory becomes a focus of political and educational struggle. How we remember matters because it informs our existence in the present and our vision of the future. Considered in this context, memory is the means by which we gain self-consciousness about the origins of our "common sense" beliefs. This self-consciousness applies not only to individuals but to institutions as well.

For example, the collective memory of teachers is important in helping them determine their collective professional purpose. If American teachers buy into a right-wing construction of an educational past where little red schoolhouses flourished with dedicated students, proud and supportive communities, and well-compensated teachers promoting "real learning" through lessons derived from blue-back spellers and McGuffey Readers, then progressive educational reforms come to be seen as "liberal meddling" with a sound system of schooling. Such a memory would induce teachers to get back to basics as soon as possible so that American greatness can be revived. Understanding as he does that the future of American education is embedded within our historical memory, Allison explodes this Disneyesque Frontierland past.

Having as a graduate student sat in Allison's history of education classes, I am familiar with his unique ability to challenge our educational memory. Blessed with a Southerner's talent for telling a story and telling it well, Allison breathes life into a field that could be deadening. Charged with an attempt to provide beginning students of American educational history with an accessible and yet sophisticated treatment of that topic, Allison never lets us down. The history presented here is never naive in relation to the way power works to privilege those already privileged and punish those already dispossessed; at the same time, however, it refuses to give up hope on the power of education to ennoble and enlighten. Indeed, Allison's faith, his sense of possibility leaves its imprint on every chapter.

Allison knows that American schools have been consistently employed by the powerful to maintain the status quo—they are, after all, cheaper than the police. At the same time, he admonishes us to remember that purpose does not dictate outcome; even in the most oppressive system literacy cannot be contained, school leaders cannot dictate what students will read in their private moments. He understands the long history of constraints on teacher creativity and autonomy, the local school board and administrative policies designed to restrict teacher prerogative in the classroom. At the same time Allison understands the long tradition of heroic teachers who have subverted such policies in the effort to assert their own professionalism and to open the minds of their students. *Present and Past* is always an ambiguous history, one that recognizes the complexity and contradictions of power and its relation to the lived worlds of students and teachers of every era.

As the author uncovers dangerous educational memories, he confronts head on the American discomfort with questions of socio-economic class. In a society that sees itself as classless, recognition not only of class differences but their social and educational impact seems almost distasteful. Similarly, Americans are quick to deny the existence of racism. In her book, *The Social Construction of Whiteness*, Ruth Frankenberg maintains that white Americans have constructed a color-evasive and power-evasive mode of thinking about race and class. This strategy suppresses the existence of white privilege rendering it invisible; whiteness thus becomes an unnamed norm by which everyone else is measured and into which others are expected to fit. When these "others" do not measure up or don't fit, they are viewed as not simply different but deficient. Allison carefully traces these dynamics in his historical exploration of social class bias and racism.

Aware of the many avenues power travels, Allison analyzes the ravages of gender bias on the educational terrain. Tracing the threat that changing perceptions of women presented to the patriarchal order, he devotes special attention to the history of women educators. The notion of women as professional self-directed educators directly conflicted with men's attachment to women as passive, subordinate social actors. Given the preponderance of women in the teaching profession, gender bias has exerted a disproportionately pernicious effect on schooling in America. Since most teachers are women, the status of teachers in general is directly tied to the status of women. Given such a reality, Allison maintains that all teachers should be feminists.

We find that our teacher education students, especially those raised in the white, upper-middle class dominant culture, sometimes encounter initial difficulty with our classes because they are hard-pressed to understand that schools may be used for non-academic or anti-democratic purposes. Understanding this tendency, Allison exposes the contradictions of a number of educational practices: tracking–promoted as a method for more effective learning but played out as a means for reproducing class, race, and gender inequalities; local control of schooling–represented as one of the greatest manifestations of American democracy but actualized by elite (doctors, bankers, lawyers, business executives) control of local schools; educational reforms–promoted as democratic campaigns for excellence but instituted as attempts to adjust future workers to an unjust workplace and an undemocratic economic system. Allison deftly contextualizes such contradictions in every chapter.

As *Present and Past* illustrates, Allison is a master teacher deeply concerned with democracy, social justice, and the reform of teacher education. His commitment and passion have already inspired many of us–this book will introduce Allison's pedagogy to a wider circle of students and teachers in their first exposure to the analysis of American educational history. We are honored to publish Allison's book in Lang's Counterpoints series. As usual we thank all the people at Lang, especially Michael Flameni whose courage and vision have made this series possible.

Preface

I wrote this book for public school teachers, a very particular audience. It is a conversation, even if a tad one sided, between teachers and me. Others are welcome to listen in and kibitz from the sidelines, but if this book were written for another audience, doctoral students or colleagues in the history of education, as examples, it would be a very different book and less fun to write. Indeed, a major difficulty in writing this book was to ignore other potential audiences while concentrating on conversations with teachers. Frequently the face of a colleague friend (or, more frightening, a colleague critic) would loom just off the computer screen with unspoken questions: "Isn't that an over-simplification?" "Why have you ignored some of the literature on that issue?" Or, more disturbing, "Why haven't you included my analysis of that issue?" I had to get rid of them by explaining: "I am not writing this book for you. Go away!" Most of the time they went.

Part of my concern in writing for teachers rather than for specialists involves language. Contemporary social theorists, including postmodernists, tend to use a very specialized language that is difficult, if not incomprehensible, for the uninitiated. In writing for you, I have tried to use everyday language, even at the risk of having ideas seem commonplace. It seems to me that if we really care about our interpretations, we should want them to be understood.

My aim in this book is not to provide a comprehensive history of education or even a survey of such a history. Rather, my objective is to provide historical perspectives on some important contemporary issues in American schooling, thus the title: *Present and Past*. I am influenced by several notions about the nature of history. The first is that a major purpose for the study of history is to escape from its clutches, to liberate ourselves from the past. As William Faulkner explained: "There is no such thing really as was, because the past is." The point is that who we are as humans, our very concept of reality, is determined by our histories, by what the past has handed down to us. And those who are most ignorant of their history are the most controlled by it because they are the least likely to understand the sources of their beliefs. They are the most likely to confuse their inherited prejudices with Truth. A second notion about history, particularly history of education, that affects the writing of this book is that popular beliefs about the past are badly distorted because people tend to compare a resented present with an idealized past. Conservatives, particularly, are likely to find a mythical golden age in the past when children were literate and well-mannered, teachers were learned and motivated only by a sense of service, and everyone was eager to be Americanized into a superior culture. It would not make much difference that this "golden age" never existed if history were not a policy study, if our beliefs about the past didn't affect decisions about schools today. But our sense of the past does influence present policies, and teachers must liberate themselves from the advice of those who would attempt to solve real problems with lessons from fantasy histories. Finally, this book is based on the premise that history (and knowledge generally) is a social construction, that by its very nature, history is subjective. There is no True history.

Because I believe that no one story is the true story, in addition to my voice in this book you will hear many voices telling stories from a number of viewpoints. There are references to other historians, and, in some cases, extended discussions of their interpretations. These discussions of the interpretations of others is a deliberate effort to acknowledge that authoritative knowledge and postmodern thinking are incompatible.

I hope this book is fair to the people and events discussed. Part of me would even like for it to be judicious. It is certainly not objective or neutral; it is biased. We often have to take sides. In this book and in life, I try to take the victim's side. My bias is for social justice, for those who have limited influence and social position, rather than for the privileged.

My debts occurred in writing this book are greater than I can possibly acknowledge. I am grateful to those who read drafts of the manuscript: Eleanor Hilty, Joe Kincheloe, David Mielke, Joe Newman, Lisa Pollard, and Beth Ann Frederick, my daughter. Their advice improved the book, and I don't doubt that it would have been better had I followed more of their counsel. I owe a special debt to Robert Cothran who drew the cover illustration. I hope you will take some time before and after reading the book to see the ways that his art reflects the themes of *Present and Past.* I wish to acknowledge Sue Carey and Charlotte Duncan who proofread the manuscript and struggled good naturally, but not always successfully, to keep me from straying too far from standard English. And, Claudia Allison remains my supporter and critic.

I

Purposes of Education: What Are Public Schools for Anyway?

Your work as American public school teachers is difficult, complicated, and frustrating for many reasons, including a lack of agreement about the purposes of public schools. A common lament is that public schools are expected to do too much—teach sex education, proper eating habits, driving skills, and wholesome values, among many other social purposes, as well as basic academic skills and knowledge of the disciplines among intellectual purposes. Read the "Teacher's Litany" of expectations for the public schools by the former Superintendent of Education in Arizona in the document reproduced below. If you are a beginning teacher, such a list probably seems both ludicrous and overwhelming. But the number of things schools are asked to do is not the major problem; the appropriateness of many of the expectations is the most significant source of conflict.

Teacher's Litany

As summarized by former Arizona Superintendent of Public Instruction Carolyn Warner, teachers in the public schools in America are expected to: Give specialized instruction for the hard of hearing, the blind, the developmentally disabled, the mentally challenged, and the gifted; develop special programs for at-risk students; build respect for the worth and dignity of the individual; do eye testing; schedule inoculations; assist in bladder control; keep health records and age certification data; attend faculty/grade/department meetings; attend professional workshops; work on an advanced degree; volunteer to supervise extra-curricula activities; participate in fund-raising; collect money to rebuild the Statue of Liberty; stress the prevention of drug, alcohol, and tobacco abuse; promote physical fitness and good nutrition habits; eradicate head lice; inculcate morals, ethics, and values; maintain order and teach self-control to the undisciplined children of undisciplined parents; provide pregnancy counseling; monitor restrooms, playgrounds, hallways, parking lots, and the cafeteria; discourage food fights; break up fist fights; pray that there are no knife fights; develop individual and civic responsibility; eliminate gender bias and sex discrimination; promote ethnic and racial tolerance; develop an appreciation of other people and other cultures; protect civil rights; help develop political know-how; teach sex education and AIDS prevention; provide suicide counseling; give First Aid instruction; train students in pulmonary-coronary resuscitation; teach the principles of free enterprise; teach management of money, property, and resources, assist in career planning; develop skills for entry into a specific field; teach etiquette and telephone manners; do job placement; serve hot breakfasts and lunches; dispense surplus milk; teach driver training; stress bicycle, automobile, and pedestrian safety; keep up with the latest trends and developments in education and be ever ready to implement these new programs; know the latest education "buzz" words; assist with bilingual language development; instruct in speed reading; encourage metric education; promote computer literacy; purchase enlightenment materials with your own money; counsel students with small problems; counsel students with major problems; protect student privacy; communicate with parents; detect and report child abuse; follow due process procedures; unteach the 4 food groups; teach the pyramid; announce that broccoli is good; build patriotism and loyalty to the ideals of democracy; encourage an understanding of the heritage of our country; develop the ability to reason; promote curiosity and a thirst for life-long learning; develop skills in the use of leisure time; build a feeling of self-worth and self-respect; teach pride in work; avoid religion; and teach reading, writing, and arithmetic.

A study of the goals of American schools was conducted by John I. Goodlad for his comprehensive book on public education, *A Place Called School.*[1] Goodlad, Director of the Center for Educational Renewal and former Dean of the Graduate School of Education, University of California at Los Angeles, is a powerful member of America's educational establishment. Goodlad and his research associates examined goal statements from all of the states and from a number of school districts. They found considerable similarity among these documents, and their historical study of state guidelines showed little change over the past half-century. A typical goal statement begins with "a philosophic preamble extolling the virtues of education" and is followed by a list of traits to be developed in the individual. Particular attention is directed towards the need to develop basic skills and "fundamental learning processes."[2] He looked for, but often failed to find, goals related to global understandings and aesthetic development.

His major disappointment, however, was the lack of a clear, explicit mandate. "There is something for everyone in the materials prepared by states," he observes. He complains that the statements "lack precision, clarity, and a ring of authority. Neither state nor district officials come out loud and clear as to what our schools are for and how they intend to fulfill these commitments."[3]

Most school administrators and education policy makers probably share Goodlad's frustration at the lack of authoritative goals for public schools. But they may also underestimate the centrality of pluralism in the postmodern world. People want different things from schooling. If there were clear, precise, authoritative goals for public schools, these goals would represent the wishes of some persons much more closely than those of others. In the political processes to create such goals, some would win and others would lose; inevitably, race, class, and gender would influence, if not determine, the winners and the losers.

Nothing that I write here should be construed as support for a position that Americans should attempt to reach a consensus about what the purposes of public schools should be; such a

position is, in my view, naive. Different viewpoints about the purposes of education often reflect differences in basic values—differences in the most fundamental ways in which people view the world and the meaning of a good life in it. Value differences are inherent and essential in a society that is both pluralistic and democratic. These basic differences cannot be concealed successfully by resorting to ambiguous language, although such a tactic may be thought by administrators and politicians to be necessary in order to gain political support for school programs. You and other teachers must be sophisticated enough to understand that a consensus on school goals is necessarily more apparent than real. Indeed, postmodernism recognizes that evidence and argument cannot be used to find the "correct" goals for public schools. Since we believe in democracy in education, we should cherish the many different voices calling for different purposes for schools.

In arguing for goal statements for schools, Goodlad acknowledges some virtue in their traditional vagueness: "They provide a common sense of direction but also some room for interpretation and adaptation to meet varying local circumstances."[4] But the reference to geography ("local circumstances") masks the heterogeneous nature of American communities. Most of us have a mental picture (with varying degrees of distortion) of polyglot neighborhoods in urban America, but many city dwellers think of rural areas as homogeneous with most of the inhabitants sharing core values and aspirations for their children. This view is also usually a distortion. Imagine with me the population of a rural county, say in Georgia. There are African-Americans (some sharecropping land on which their ancestors were slaves, some newly returned to the South after generations in Detroit and Cleveland, some physicians and attorneys, some unemployed), white Americans (some families living on the same land since the eighteenth century, some transplanted Yankees), and a few-but-growing number of Asians. There are thousands of Southern Baptists (disagreeing about practically everything), Roman Catholics (some of whom don't practice birth control), Episcopalians, Presbyterians, assorted evangelicals, fundamentalists, Pentecostals, charismatics, a number of doubters, a few dozen quiet unbelievers, and one Neo-Druid.

There are rich farmers, poor farmers, peanut farmers, and marijuana farmers. There are political reactionaries (some belonging to the KKK), a majority of conservatives, a number of frustrated liberals, and a few radicals (including two self-admitted Marxists). There are women who accept their low status in a patriarchal society as the natural order of things, and there are a growing number of feminists. And so it goes. The people of this local community want a good education for their children; they will have a devil of a time agreeing about what that means.

School administrators and policy makers may be overly concerned with goal *statements* (which is not to say that they are overly concerned with goals). Teachers, having their own goals for the subjects they teach, often pay little attention to such statements. Even when there is apparent agreement on at least the major goals of schools among citizens, the meanings that people attach to goal statements do not simply vary, they are often conflicting and irreconcilable. The result is that the meaning of even a carefully worded goal may become the source of tension and conflict in a community.

Civic Purposes of Education

Since one of the most commonly stated purposes of public schools is to prepare "good" citizens, I will use this goal to illustrate the problem. Support for civic education is widespread but not unanimous–some persons argue that public schools should not have the responsibility or even the right to deliberately and systematically inculcate values, including civic values. However, almost all schools have goal statements related to citizenship; development of patriotism and participation in government is often emphasized. The pedestrian-worded goal statement of my local school system reads: "Become an informed citizen who participates in all levels of government."[5]

Even if people in a community can agree on a general goal statement about preparing good citizens, their expectations about what will be taught is often the subject of controversy. (Imagine how differently the citizens of our rural Georgia county might view the meaning of good citizenship.)

Conservatives, including members of "patriotic" societies such as the American Legion and the Daughters of the American Revolution, often want unquestioning and uncritical nationalistic sentiments instilled into the young. They expect schools to require students to engage in patriotic exercises including saluting the flag, singing of the national anthem, and having assemblies with local and imported Americanism speakers. They may not want "my country right or wrong" to be the basis of civic education, but they want emphasis on what is right with America; and they want teachers and textbooks to ignore or minimize social and economic problems, past and present.

Liberals, on the other hand, grapple with the dilemma of preparing good citizens by teaching common or shared values in a pluralistic society. One of America's most distinguished educational historians, R. Freeman Butts, has spent the years since his retirement in 1975 from Teachers College, Columbia, campaigning for citizenship education (he calls it civic learning or civism) in the public schools. His goal is typically liberal: to integrate in the school curriculum "cohesive elements" of a cosmopolitan view of America with the values of "stable pluralism." In his ideal civic learning, differences among peoples would be honored and respected at the same time shared values would be emphasized.[6]

A radical citizenship education encourages students and teachers to critically examine public and private institutions (Congress, television, business, churches, their own school, etc.) for evidence of failures to foster social justice. More complex understandings of the nature of racism, sexism, and social class bias in America are objectives. The development of more sophisticated intellectual skills–the ability to recognize slogans and propaganda for younger students, the ability to deconstruct hidden ideologies for older ones–are also goals of radical educators.

These incompatible purposes for citizenship education are only examples of the lack of consensus on the goals of public schools. Reflect on how adherents of these three political ideologies might differ on other purposes of schools: economic education, sex education, or even aesthetic education.

Historical Perspectives

We will now examine some purposes of schools in the American past in order to gain a historical perspective on the aims of education. Most of my examples will come from two periods that are of particular interest to educational historians: seventeenth-century Puritan New England and the common school movement of the mid-nineteenth century. But I will occasionally give examples from other periods and even provide a short hypothetical (that is imaginary) case study from pre-history.

In seventeenth-century colonial America, the primary goals of schooling, as set by the ruling class, were conservative. In his classic study of American education, Merle Curti observed that colonial schools were "instruments for the preservation of religious faith and existing economic and social arrangements."[7] I suspect that you are not surprised at this purpose for schooling. In our more secular society today, most leaders might want to substitute political arrangements for religious faith, but the use of schools to preserve the place, privileges, and ideologies of the elite remains a powerful (but unstated and usually unexamined) goal of schools.

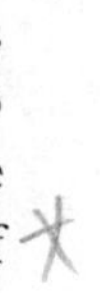

By their very nature, schools have conservative aims. (Of course, aims and outcomes are quite different things, a point I will return to in the conclusion of this chapter.) Imagine with me the purpose of the first school in human pre-history, that is, the first attempt to consciously, deliberately, and systematically teach the young. Standing outside their cave in their bear skins (or in their bare skins if your imagination runs in that direction), one leader of the clan turns to another and says: "These damn kids are going astray. They are not learning the right stuff. Their parents are too permissive. We had better have some rules about what they must be taught." (Admittedly, this is a loose translation.)

Perhaps the most influential educational philosopher in ancient history, Plato, urged this same goal of education on rulers, parents, and teachers. Don't even allow your children to play games different from the games their fathers played, he warned, because if they play different games, they will want different institutions and laws.

Religious Purposes

American educational historians argue about whether or not the roots of our public schools can be found in colonial America, particularly in the "Old Deluder Satan Act" passed in 1647 Massachusetts. I suspect that most of you can control your enthusiasm for hearing more about this debate, but the law is important because it was among the first to require the establishment of schools in the English-speaking world, and the arguments supporting its passage can provide perspectives on the goals of schools. Indeed, many of the goals of seventeenth-century New England schools remain goals of public schools today, although they may be unstated and perhaps even hidden from the consciousness of some teachers who adopt them in day-to-day practice.

A major purpose of the law was religious, and religion permeated the schools. The preamble to the law reads, "It being the chief project of the old deluder Satan to keep men from a knowledge of the Scriptures." The schools established by the law were to teach the young to read English so they could perform their sacred duty, reading the Bible. After 1701, schoolmasters were required to have the approval of three ministers before they could be hired. Much time in school was spent in prayer, Bible reading, and in memorization of whatever catechism had the approval of the town minister. The students were required to attend and sit together in church under the watchful eye of the schoolmaster. And, in some towns, it was traditional for the minister to go to school on Monday morning to examine the students on their understanding of the previous day's sermon.

The purposes of schools under the "Old Deluder Satan Act" were based, in part, on seventeenth-century Puritan views about the nature of children. Recent historians have revised some traditional beliefs about Puritans' views of children (including challenging the idea that Puritans saw children only as miniature adults). They also warn us that the advice of leading Puritan ministers may not have been followed in practice, as the advice of authorities in child rearing may not represent actual practice by parents today.[8] But, in this chapter, we are concerned with the educational goals of the powerful voices in society, and, in seventeenth-century New England, these were often the ministers. They taught the doctrine of original sin. All persons were by their very nature evil, sharing in the sin of Adam and Eve. Children were no exception; they might look cute and innocent, but, as Cotton Mather wrote in *A Family Well-Ordered* (1699), they "were born in sin and were creatures of Hell, Death, and Wrath and therefore had corrupt natures."[9] They were "depraved, unregenerate, and damned" and, as minister John Robinson argued, they had to be broken so they could be taught "humility and tractableness," a process that might start with one- and two-year-olds.[10] This view of children was consistent with reliance on the whipping post, a standard feature of colonial schools. Generations of teachers (and parents) were admonished that if children were full of the wrath of hell, they obviously need the hell beaten out of them; if they were full of the Devil, they needed the devil beaten out of them. However, even in the colonial period there were strong differences of opinion among parents about childrearing. The evangelicals, who felt that they were led by God to break the wills of children "through rigorous physical, verbal, and emotional punishment," were challenged by "moderates," who represented the majority of parents in the eighteenth century.[11] But many could accept the conventional wisdom of the strict Calvinist: a happy child was a sinning child. I suspect that most of us have experienced at least a teacher or two who seemed to subscribe to these seventeenth-century Puritan purposes for schools.

In today's public schools, it would be impossible, I suspect, to find a textbook that reflects the goals of education as well as the *New England Primer* did in colonial America. This textbook was first printed in 1690 and was used, in a number of different editions, for well over a hundred years. From the learning of the alphabet by rhyming couplets—"In Adam's Fall, We Sinned All"—to the learning of words of four syllables—"benevolence, everlasting, fidelity, glorifying"—the purpose of the *Primer* was explicitly religious, to prepare youth to live in a biblical commonwealth. But the *Primer* was also full of reminders that this life is short, and death is always waiting for us. What do you think of the following poem for young children?

I in the Burning Place may see
Graves shorter there than I;
From Death's Arrest no Age is free,
Young Children too may die:
My God, may such an awful sight
Awakening be to me!
Oh! that by early Grace I might
For Death prepared be.[12]

It's hardly "Kathy Visits the Zoo" or something similar that we might find for the same-age child today. Paul Ford, an early twentieth-century historian of the *Primer,* concluded his sympathetic study of the religious purposes of this book with, "It taught millions to read, and not one to sin."[13]

The goal of inculcating Protestant Christian beliefs in public-school children continued through the eighteenth and nineteenth centuries. Despite Supreme Court decisions, this purpose persists in many public school classrooms today. In the middle of the nineteenth century, the most popular schoolbook, selling over twenty million copies, was Webster's *Elementary Speller,* affectionately known (by those who no longer had to read it) as "old-blue back." The Christian message was explicit: ". . . the devil is the great adversary of man. We are apt to live forgetful of our continual dependence on God, and it should never be forgotten that it is a solemn thing to die and appear before him for judgement."[14]

In her study of nineteenth-century textbooks, *Guardians of Tradition,* Ruth Miller Elson demonstrates that schoolbooks were not just Protestant; they were also anti-Catholic. "No theme in these textbooks before 1870, is more universal than anti-Catholicism."[15] She quotes a "typical treatment" from a 1828 reader:

> For many ages the Popes not only pretended to be infallible, but exalted themselves above all the kings of the earth, to the very throne of CHRIST; assuming the right of pardoning sin, and of giving or rather selling the liberty of indulging in every species of wickedness and corruption.[16]

Not surprisingly, the virulent anti-Catholicism of public schools drove Roman Catholics in America from public schools, causing them to create separate, parochial school systems.

Public schools in the nineteenth and early twentieth centuries were supported enthusiastically by evangelical Christians because these schools inculcated unabashedly their beliefs in children.[17] Today, evangelical Christians are often among the most bitter critics of public schools. They feel betrayed by the pluralistic nature of the curriculum with its emphasis on multiculturalism, including attempts to foster respect for different religious traditions. They resent what they perceive as a lack of balance in portrayals of men and women in traditional and non-traditional gender roles. They are appalled by what they perceive as pornography masquerading as sex education, particularly in the presentation of birth control information and in AIDS education. They are angered by Supreme Court decisions disallowing public prayer and other religious exercises under the auspices of public schools. And, above all, they are infuriated by what they perceive as condescending attitudes of school personnel and curriculum makers toward their basic values and religious beliefs. Like the Catholics of a previous generation, many have taken their children from the public schools and are sending them to Christian day schools. Not surprisingly, they are among the most enthusiastic supporters of former President Bush's and Secretary of Education Alexander's proposal for a voucher system which would allow public funds to be spent to support children in private and parochial schools.

The Transmission of the Cultural Heritage

The religious goals for schooling in seventeenth-century New England may have been paramount, but there were other aims, some of which remain important today. One of the most persistent purposes of education is to pass on the best of the cultural heritage. Today there is endless and sometimes mean-spirited debate about what the best of our heritage means, a point I will return to at the end of this section. In the colonies and throughout Christendom at the time, the best of the cultural heritage was thought to be Latin and Greek philosophy and literature—the classical curriculum. The Old Deluder Satan Act not only required towns to hire a schoolmaster to teach children to read the Bible and other Christian literature, it required the larger towns (those of over one hundred families) to hire a master to teach Latin grammar. Historian Samuel Eliot Morison, a descendent of the Puritans and an apologist for them, writes with warm approval of this purpose of schooling. In majestic prose, Morison praises the Puritan's devotion to this purpose of schools:

> It was no small feat to keep alive the tradition of classical antiquity in a region that had never known the grandeur that was Rome, the glory that was Greece. The New England schools and colleges did just that: and handed down a priceless classical tradition to the eighteenth and nineteenth centuries.[18]

The teaching of classical learning, according to Morison, was an end in itself. The leaders of the colony (a remarkable number of them university graduates) had received a classical education. If we are persons of power, we tend to think that the type of education we received is the most valuable kind of education possible. After all, look what it did for us. But that is only part of the reason that classical learning was so strongly supported in the American wilderness.

The Puritans did not come to the New World in order to become Americans. They were not in rebellion against European, particularly English, culture. Indeed, James Axtell, in his excellent history of colonial New England education, *The School Upon a Hill*, refers to the colonists as the New English.[19] Perched on the rocky Atlantic seacoasts with a wilderness stretching on forever behind them, they were fearful about what was to happen to their children and the generations that were to come after them. Native people were a special source of anxiety. Not only did they present real physical dangers, particularly after 1675 with the outbreak of King Philip's War, but the very existence of these "savages" with their long hair, barbarous manners, and undisciplined life in the woods (all of this from the perspective of the Puritans, of course) presented an alternative way of life that chilled the hearts of parents like posters of heavy metal stars do to the parents of fourteen-year-olds today. They, like the cave people mentioned before, wanted to systematically instruct the young in order to pass on the traditional way of life.

A traditional curriculum, whatever form it may take from place to place or from time to time, has as one of its purposes the protection of the young from whatever barbarians may be lurking around. For the "New English," the elegant languages and venerable wisdom of the ancients, refined by Christianity, were an attempt to pass on the best of the European heritage to youths who would live near the allure of the wilderness.

My study of schools on the middle-western frontier showed much the same phenomena. The fear of cultural degeneration was strong among the first families on the edge of the frontier; they were anxious to establish schools. Once their log cabins had been replaced by clapboard houses with glass windows and the landscape was of farms rather than forests, they often became less apprehensive about the schooling of their children; the crisis had passed.[20]

When statewide systems of public schools were created in the mid-nineteenth century, they were called common schools. The conservative leaders of American society at the time were fearful of new immigrants to America, particularly the Irish whom they saw as ignorant, superstitious, and often depraved and overly sensuous. They, and other alien groups, had to be taught proper values to be Americanized. Historians debate whether the Anglo-Saxon Protestants who controlled American institutions were afraid of divisiveness in society caused by cultural differences or if they just abhorred pluralism. Regardless, they supported common schools to teach all children an idealized common Protestant heritage, even though anti-Catholicism doomed such common schools to failure.

Is the passing on of the cultural heritage in order to protect youth from barbarism still an important purpose of American schools? And if so, who are the late twentieth-century barbarians? Surely, you said yes to the first question. Parents, teachers, and societal leaders expect schools to inculcate in children and adolescents the "best" of our human heritage. But who are the barbarians who are lurking in our late-twentieth-century "jungles"? Barbarism like beauty is often in the mind of the beholder; but, for many middle and upper middle-class Americans, barbarism is found in popular culture, particularly in youth culture. Adults are often appalled and terrified at what they perceive as popular lifestyles that are both degenerate and seductive. The message that parents, grandparents, and other adults overhear from "youth-oriented" media and music is to engage in easy and perverted sex, to do illicit drugs, and to become involved in other destructive behavior. Responses from these adults range from appeals for religious revivals, to demands for censorship, to cries for tougher punishment (including use of capital punishment) for drug dealers and "merchants of filth." Well-schooled, upper-middle-class Americans especially have faith that the passing on of the best of the cultural heritage remains a civilizing influence.

While many Americans think that the teaching of the social sciences and humanities is primarily for the purpose of college preparation, others see their paramount purpose as providing superior or "elevated" examples of values, tastes, and heroes. What have we accomplished, they ask, by providing most Americans with functional literacy if they only read the tabloids from the supermarket checkout lines with such headlines as "BIGFOOT DELIVERED MY BABY," "MY DOG IS AN ALIEN," or "HITLER IS ADVISOR TO ARAB LEADERS." Assignments on William Shakespeare, Mark Twain, or even Robert Cormier are attempts to keep the barbarians at bay.

Another example is music. The advocates of high culture as curriculum hope that "good" music programs in schools will act as an antidote to the poison (sold without even warning labels they complain) that kills musical taste. Beethoven, Handel, and Mozart are sent to do battle with Guns N' Roses or, in other subcultures, Snoop Doggy Dogg or Willie and Reba.

I have a fantasy about this purpose of education. I am teaching a class of senior education students when a giant vacuum-cleaner hose sucks us up into a space ship and carries us to a planet far, far away and leaves us forever to our own devices. (As in all good fantasies, the setting is subtropical with palm trees and perhaps even a blue lagoon.) The students begin to have children—after proper marriage rituals and ceremonies, of course. And after five or six years, I am chained to a palm tree, with only a water dish, under orders to recreate verbatim the American history textbooks from which I used to teach. These new parents are anxious that their children learn about George

Washington and Abraham Lincoln, hear the stories of Nathaniel Hawthorne and Mark Twain, and perhaps even sing "Camptown Races." Like our mythical cave people, Plato, and the Puritans, they are dreadfully afraid that their children will grow up different from them and that these differences will mean rejection of their values and way of life. The thought that their grandchildren might be strangers is terrifying to these parents in their new paradise and to most other people as well.

Our society is engaged in an emotional (often angry and bitter) debate about what the cultural heritage is that should be passed on. Conservatives insist that there are great books and great music that have stood the test of time and should be part of the cultural legacy of all Americans, that quotes and ideas from Shakespeare, Milton, Emerson, and the Bible provide cultural counters that allow us to understand each other. This position is popularized by best-selling books such as E. D. Hirch's *Cultural Literacy* and Allan Bloom's *The Closing of the American Mind*. Many African-Americans, Native Americans, and other minorities as well as feminists object, arguing that this cultural heritage is the heritage of only a minority of Americans: those who are primarily white, male, and Christian. Those who object to this passing on of the "best" of the cultural heritage argue that it is a means of social control, that children and youth are taught that the proper ways of perceiving the world are white and male centered. If young women or minority children see a different reality, they are somehow deviant and had better "shape up" if they want to succeed in American culture.

Minorities and feminists often argue for a multicultural curriculum which will broaden the public school curriculum to include the literature, history, and music of groups other than those who represent the power elite in society. As teachers, you will continually be making decisions that support one or another of these positions; it is unavoidable.

The Economic Purposes of Education

During the 1980s, the emphasis was on the economic purposes of education, almost to the exclusion of anything else. In keeping with the spirit of that decade, the preoccupation with accumulating and flaunting of wealth, the national education reform reports of the 1980s–*A Nation At Risk* (1983), *Action for Excellence* (1983), and *A Nation Prepared: Teachers for the 21st Century* (1986)–stressed that the purpose of public schools was production of human capital. With the support of Presidents Reagan and Bush and Secretaries of Education Bennett and Alexander, the campaign to convince Americans that public schools were, in large part, responsible for our failures to compete economically with Japan and Western Europe was remarkably successful. In the final decade of the twentieth century, a more productive work force seems to be our national leaders' paramount goal of schooling. The advocates of human capital theory argue that intellectual abilities and academic skills, particularly in mathematics and sciences, become more and more important for national prosperity in a world economy increasingly based on technology.

There are other economic purposes for schooling that will be examined in this section. Historically, more emphasis has been placed on using schools to train a docile work force by stressing respect for authority, regular attendance, and a high tolerance for boredom than on mass schooling for intellectual growth. As Joel Spring points out in his history of education since 1945, *The Sorting Machine*, public schools have served the needs of supplying American business with workers by sorting individuals into different occupational paths, using such techniques as career education curricula and guidance counselors. Spring calls them professional sorters. In chapters five and six, I discuss the social-class, race, and ethnic-group bias that operates when schools sort students into different tracks.[21]

The economic purposes of schooling that I have discussed so far serve the interests of business and industry. Public schools are also supposed to serve the economic needs of individuals by helping them develop the knowledge, skills, and attitudes necessary for vertical mobility in the American class structure. The idea that education pays in dollars and cents is now commonplace; it is part of the conventional wisdom of our society. Historian David Tyack writes that "there is little evidence, however, that citizens in the nineteenth century thought this way about schooling."[22] Until the twentieth century, the paramount aims of schools were civic and moral education. When there were arguments about the economic benefits of schooling, the stress was placed on the importance of developing character traits that would lead to prosperity, such as punctuality, regularity, and reliability.[23]

But even in the colonial period, clergy, who may have wanted schools primarily for religious reasons, appealed to the economic interests of the wealthier members of society who had the power to pass and enforce school legislation. Part of the appeal was that investment in education pays off in the general prosperity of the community. Early in the eighteenth century, Thomas Bray, a missionary for the wonderfully named Society for the Propagation of the Gospel in Foreign Parts, based his appeals for support of schools on the theory that education pays. "Without education it is impossible to preserve the spirit of commerce," he argues, because "in a word, commerce and riches are the offspring of industry and unprecarious property; but these depend on virtue and liberty, which again depend on knowledge and religion."[24]

In their attempts to convince the wealthy that support for education for the poor was a good investment, the colonial clergy preached a doctrine of social control: that schools would indoctrinate the young in "proper" values, including respect for their betters and an acceptance of the justice of the social and economic system. The wealthy were promised that the right instruction would "make the restless, wretched, and often well-nigh unmanageable underlings more temperate, more industrious, more virtuous, in short more content with their station" in life.[25] In every generation, advocates of schooling have had to make similar appeals to the politically powerful in order to garner financial support for schooling.

In the campaign to establish public school systems in the mid-nineteenth century, Horace Mann and the other leaders of the common school movement again appealed to the owning class. Industrialization was underway, and the public school promoters made explicit promises, in Michael B. Katz's words, "to train and discipline an urban and industrial workforce." Workers were to be inculcated in "modern habits of punctuality, regularity, docility, and the postponement of gratification." It was not an accident "that the mass production of clocks and watches began at about the same time as the mass production of public schools."[26]

Public school systems in the South lagged behind. But, in the first decade of the twentieth century, the southern education campaigns to establish working public school systems in the South were underway, and the southern progressives who led the campaigns supported vigorously the human capital purpose for public schooling. This aim of education was powerfully articulated by a leader of that movement, Walter Hines Page, journalist and later diplomat. In 1904, he insisted that:

> The proper standard to judge men by is an economic standard, not an academic one. . . . One untrained white man or one untrained worthless negro [sic] may cause trouble throughout a whole county. For this reason it is important to train the child of every hill-billy [sic], of every politician, of every negro [sic] in Alabama. In every case it is an economic reason, not a merely personal reason, not a race reason, not a class reason. In an ideal economic state, if we were to construct it as ruthlessly as Plato constructed his ideal Republic, we should kill every untrained man; for he is in the way. He is a burden, and he brings down the level of the economic efficiency of the whole community.[27]

Another common economic argument for schooling in our time is that schooling is a good investment because the proper kind of education will keep the poor off the welfare rolls. Again, similar appeals were made in colonial America. The Old Deluder Satan Act of 1647 was not just protection against "the fiery Darts of Satan," it "also obliged parents to train their children in useful trades lest, by becoming paupers, they should become burdens to the well-to-do community."[28]

Of course, the economic rewards of schooling are not just prosperity for the whole community or additional wealth for the already well-to-do; education should pay off for persons (even for those born poor) who stay in school and are diligent in their studies. With growing secularization and commercialization in the society in the late eighteenth and early nineteenth centuries, more emphasis was placed on education for individual economic success. For ambitious white males with the proper attitudes and values ("virtues of industry, frugality, and prudence"), America was indeed a land of opportunity.[29]

Opportunities were, of course, much less promising for Native American and African-American men and all women.

It is fitting that Benjamin Franklin (whom historians sometimes call "the first American" because he so exemplified the traits and characteristics that are associated with middle-class Americans) was both symbol and advocate of the American tradition of advocating a practical education for material success. Although Franklin proposed reforms in schools, particularly more utilitarian studies at the expense of Latin and Greek, he (ever holding up the model of the "self-made man"—as exemplified by himself) stressed learning lessons from experience. His *Poor Richard's Almanack* constantly admonished "that life itself could be a continuing education," and in the "business of living, the greatest profits accrued to those who learned most diligently."[30]

As society became more secular, this economic purpose of schooling began to compete strongly with religious aims. A late nineteenth-century historian of the *New England Primer*, Paul Leicester Ford, lamented "worldly" changes in that book that would "have made the true Puritan turn in his grave." He was particularly unhappy with a poem about why one should learn to read that became popular in editions of the *Primer* published after 1790:

> He who ne'er learns his A. B. C.
> Forever will a blockhead be.
> But he who learns his letters fair
> Shall have a coach to take the air.[31]

With only a small translation to contemporary language, this verse has the same appeal that your parents may have made to you and that you may make to your students: stay in school and do well in your studies and you will earn financial success. You shall have a Porsche "to take the air."

Conclusion

The politically powerful in America have promoted conservative purposes for public education. Both social control and maintaining the social structure have been among their aims for schools. Based on the premise that public order is better obtained by citizens who have internalized values leading to proper behavior than by having a police state (Horace Mann, the "father" of the common schools, suggested that schools were cheaper than police), the privileged have advocated teaching traditional values as a means of keeping people behaving in prescribed ways. People who don't like this purpose for schools call it social control; people who think it positive or benign call it socialization.

Schools have also been used to prevent change in the social structure, to help the privileged maintain their place in society. According to reproduction theory, schools reproduce the inequities already existing in society; the treatment of the poor, minorities, and women in school mirrors their status in the broader society. Thus, schools have been what they were supposed to be: "guardians of tradition."

But purposes and outcomes are not the same thing. Despite the conservative nature of the aims of education, schooling has been liberating for many persons in every generation. Literacy, however obtained, tends to liberate, and ignorance leads not to bliss but to powerlessness. There are always individuals who are able to take from school what they find useful for their own intellectual growth and who can detect and reject attempts to condition them to accept views that stunt their development—they are often considered troublemakers. The phenomenon of escaping from institutional control by making conscious decisions about what to accept and what to reject, based on an individual's sense of personal integrity and needs, is called human agency.

As indicated before, American citizens do not have a consensus on the purposes of public schooling. Many persons in our society do not agree with the traditional conservative purposes for education. They take seriously other goals of schooling, including encouraging youth to capture their own vision for their lives and to develop critical intelligence so they can become responsible critics of their world. These goals are sometimes supported by teachers like Robin Williams' character, John Keating, in *Dead Poets Society*. Of course, like Keating, they are sometimes fired. But, despite the dangers, there are few schools of any size that don't have at least an underground of such teachers. You might consider (in a much less elitist institution than Keating's, I hope) the rewards and dangers of finding your own way of becoming a teacher who challenges the traditional purposes of the public schools.

Notes

1 John I. Goodlad, *A Place Called School: Prospects for the Future* (New York: McGraw-Hill, 1984).

2 *Ibid.*, p. 47.

3 *Ibid.*, pp. 48-49.

4 *Ibid.*, p. 50.

5 Knox County, Tennessee, "Goals of Education."

6 R. Freeman Butts, *The Revival of Civic Learning: A Rationale for Citizenship Education in American Schools* (Phi Delta Kappa Educational Foundation, 1980), pp. 162-163.

7 Merle Curti, *The Social Ideas of American Educators* (Totowa, NJ: Littlefield, Adams and Co., 1959 [1935]), p. 4.

8 Ross W. Beales, Jr., "The Child in Seventeenth-Century America" and Constance B. Schulz, "Children and Childhood in the Eighteenth Century," *American Childhood: A Research Guide and Historical Handbook*, eds. Joseph M. Hawes and N. Ray Hiner (Westport, CT: Greenwood Press, 1985).

9 R. Freeman Butts and Lawrence A. Cremin, *A History of Education in American Culture* (New York: Holt, Rinehart and Winston, 1953), p. 68.

10 Adolphe E. Meyer, *An Educational History of the American People* (New York: McGraw-Hill Book Company, 1967), p. 36; Beales, p. 30.

11 Schulz, p. 62.

12 Paul Leicester Ford (ed.), *The New England Primer: A History of its Origin and Development* (New York: Teachers College, Columbia University, 1962 [1897]), p. 22.

13 *Ibid.*, p. 53.

14 Curti, p. 17.

15 Ruth Miller Elson, *Guardians of Tradition: American Schoolbooks of the Nineteenth Century* (Lincoln: University of Nebraska Press, 1964), p. 53.

16 *Ibid.*, p. 48.

17 Carl E. Kaestle, *Pillars of the Republic: Common Schools and American Society, 1780-1860* (New York: Hill and Wang, 1983); David B. Tyack, *The One Best System: A History of American Urban Education* (Cambridge: Harvard University Press, 1974).

18 Samuel Eliot Morison, *The Puritan Pronaos: Studies in the Intellectual Life of New England in the Seventeenth Century* (New York: New York University Press, 1936), pp. 15-16.

19 James Axtell, *The School Upon a Hill: Education and Society in Colonial New England* (New York: W. W. Norton and Company, 1974).

20 Clinton B. Allison, "Frontier Schools: A Reflection of the Turner Hypothesis" (unpublished Ph.D. dissertation, University of Oklahoma, 1969), Chapter III.

21 Joel Spring, *The Sorting Machine: National Educational Policy Since 1945* (New York: David McKay Co., 1976).

22 David Tyack, "Ways of Seeing: An Essay on the History of Compulsory Schooling," *Harvard Educational Review*, 46 (August, 1976), p. 82.

23 *Ibid.*

24 Curti, p. 6.

25 *Ibid.*, p. 7.

26 Michael B. Katz, "The Origins of Public Education: A Reassessment," *History of Education Quarterly*, 16 (Winter, 1976), pp. 394-395.

27 Clinton B. Allison, "The Conference for Education in the South: An Exercise in *Noblesse Oblige*," *Journal of Thought*, 16 (Summer, 1981), p. 43.

28 Curti, p. 8.

29 Lawrence A. Cremin, *American Education: The Colonial Experience, 1607-1783* (New York: Harper Torchbooks, 1970), pp. 375, 387.

30 *Ibid.*, p. 388.

31 Ford, pp. 48-49.

II

The American Teacher: Why Don't Teachers Get More Respect?

The television promotion proclaims: "Teaching, the hardest job you will ever love." This recruitment slogan suggests the ambivalent feelings that many teachers have about their occupation. The rewards of teaching can be so great that teachers are willing to persevere in an occupation with many dissatisfiers. There is a common, almost universal agreement among teachers as to what is rewarding in their job: interactions with students. Dan C. Lortie in his classic sociological study, *Schoolteacher*, calls this interaction the interpersonal theme.[1] Great satisfaction comes from watching the faces of students when they understand what had been previously incomprehensible to them. The rewards are particularly great when teachers have had the creative autonomy to structure the learning situation in order to achieve this result. The teaching act itself is so rewarding that other satisfiers of the occupation such as extended vacations and job security through tenure are of considerably less importance to most teachers.

Despite the rewards of teaching, many American teachers are unhappy with their jobs. The turnover is high and, as a recent Carnegie study (*A Nation Prepared: Teachers for the 21st Century*) puts it, teaching is an "early exit occupation."[2] According to national polls, only about 20 percent of teachers "certainly would" become teachers if they were able to choose again (although 69 percent, according to Goodlad in *A Place Called School*, would still select teaching as a career.[3]) Fifty-one percent of teachers say they have "seriously considered" leaving teaching for another occupation, and, in a statistic similar to that in other states, 40 percent of the teachers in my home state of Tennessee do leave the profession during their first seven years in the classroom.[4] Many of those who stay are often dissatisfied in their work, and those who have left generally have a higher degree of satisfaction with almost every aspect of their non-teaching jobs including higher salaries, less job stress, and greater control over their work.[5] The dissatisfaction of public school teachers is hardly a secret. The polls confirm what we too frequently see in the unhappy professional lives of our spouses, children, and friends who are teachers. Yet we in colleges and schools of education, hoping to recruit some of the brightest and best into teaching, are often reluctant to treat the satisfiers and dissatisfiers of teaching realistically. I will not attempt to catalog all of the causes for teacher dissatisfaction, and I certainly will not attempt to establish a hierarchy of causes of a teacher-misery index. However, I will examine three major dissatisfiers of teachers: (a) the lack of a feeling of appreciation for their work by the public, (b) the lack of creative autonomy in their jobs, and (c) the sense of isolation from other educators. (I will address the issue of teacher pay in the next chapter.)

Teachers often feel that Americans undervalue the importance of their work, and this results in low status for their profession. Lortie agrees, calling the teacher's social position "special but shadowed":

> Teaching seems to have more than its share of status anomalies. It is honored and disdained, praised as "dedicated service" and lampooned as "easy work." It is permeated with the rhetoric of professionalism, yet features incomes below those earned by workers with considerably less education.[6]

With national attention focused on the shortcomings and failures of public schools in the last few years, teachers are getting a great deal of attention, much of it unfavorable. This negative attention exacerbates their feelings of being unappreciated. The major national reports on education of the last decade, *A Nation at Risk*, National Commission on Excellence in Education; *Action for Excellence*, Task Force on Education for Economic Growth; and *A Nation Prepared: Teachers for the 21st Century*, Carnegie Corporation, indicate shortcomings of teachers, particularly with their academic quality. With the possible exception of *A Nation at Risk*, the reports do not engage in direct teacher bashing, but teachers often feel that they are blamed for the perceived failures of the public schools. And they often feel victimized by criticisms for conditions over which they have little or no control.

In discussions about public schools, the national reports are often alluded to but seldom read. Periodicals, particularly popular magazines, are the chief source of information and opinion about the public schools for middle and upper-middle-class Americans who are interested in the issue. (And as I will explain in chapter four, it is persons in the upper-middle class whose opinions are most likely to be translated into educational policy.) News magazines in particular have devoted much attention to schools and teachers over the past decade. Without doing a library search for evidence, I have just glanced through a pile of old *Time* and *Newsweek* magazines in my study (tidiness is a nuisance rather than a virtue). In *Time* for June 16, 1980, the cover story is "Help, Teacher Can't Teach," an issue unlikely to make teachers feel good about themselves. Later issues are the November 14, 1988, *Time* with the cover story, "Who's Teaching our Children?"; and a special edition of *Newsweek* for Fall/Winter of 1990 on education with the cover story: "How to Teach Our Kids."

There is nothing new about periodical cover stories on teachers and their failures. Two examples more than a half-century apart suggest the continuity of the negative treatment. *Life* magazine in 1950 devoted a "Special Issue" to the problems of American public schools with a virulent attack on teacher education: "Who Teaches the Teachers? Their Scorned and Neglected Colleges are Appallingly Ill Equipped for the Job."[7] One of the popular magazines at the turn-of-the-century, *The Forum*, ran a series of nine issues during 1892 and 1893 exploring the evils of the public schools. The author of the articles, Joseph Mayer Rice, complained of the rigidity, coldness, and mindlessness of the schools. He was appalled by the authoritarian teachers who were "cold and unsympathetic and at times actually cruel and barbarous."[8]

A second dissatisfier of teachers is restrictions on their creative autonomy, their lack of control over time during their workday—an issue that is central to a consideration of professionalism. The greatest satisfactions of teachers come from teaching itself—from the hundreds of decisions they make each hour about instructional strategies, curriculum, and discipline. Freedom to make these creative decisions is often limited by administrators and other members of the educational bureaucracy as well as by lay boards of education. As long as state or local boards of education can require that specific subject matter be taught to every child in a prescribed way at a particular time, or as long as lay boards, consisting of say, dairy farmers, oil wildcatters, and real estate promoters, can decide which are the only acceptable textbooks and other curricular material to carry out the prescribed curriculum, teaching is not a profession.

In addition to restrictions on the practice of teaching, educational bureaucracies often assign numerous petty tasks to teachers. If teachers were treated as professionals, they would not be required to perform the tasks of janitor, police, clerk, and ticket and cookie seller. Although those who have not taught usually don't realize it, teaching loads are far too heavy without these extra, non-teaching assignments. Teachers are regularly assigned too many students for too many hours a week.

A third major dissatisfier is a teacher's isolation from other adult professionals. A teacher in many public schools is in an analogous situation with a lion tamer who is asked to spend six continuous hours alone in a cage of bored lions, putting them through their unnatural paces. The recent reform documents recognize the seriousness of the problem, although they describe it in more restrained ways. Goodlad writes of the "classroom cells" where teachers work and which are "symbols and predictive of their relative isolation from one another and from sources of ideas beyond their own background of experience." They have only "brief and casual kinds of associations" and rarely join "in collaborative endeavors."[9] *The Shopping Mall High School* discusses the need for conversations among teachers about education and students:

> It is more important to organize school time so that such conversations can occur, than to impose an ideal curriculum on schools from the out-

> side . . . rearranging school time in this manner empowers teachers by placing them in the center of educational decision making rather than on the periphery. It empowers good teachers by removing the protective isolation that allows the mediocre to survive and the competent to remain impotent.[10]

Tomorrow's Teachers, a report of the Holmes Group, a consortium of teacher educators in research universities, also discusses this sense of isolation by complaining that teachers "still spend all of their professional time alone with students, leaving little or no time for work with other adult professionals to improve their knowledge and skills."[11] Professional teachers need time "to reflect, plan, discuss . . . with their colleagues," echoes The Carnegie Forum.[12] Sixty-eight percent of Tennessee teachers report that they have little or no time to talk with colleagues about what they are doing. Seymour Sarason has found in working with teachers at his psychoeducational clinic at Yale "that teaching is often lonely, repetitive work in which a teacher is incessantly asked to give and ends the day emotionally drained."[13]

I have divided my discussion of the history of teachers into two chapters. In this chapter I examine many of the problems and inadequacies of the historical teacher, particularly, but not exclusively, in the colonial period and early nineteenth century when most teachers were men. I include widely accepted, though unfortunately often negative, images of teachers in the past, including their moral lapses and their academic limitations. I also discuss the historical teachers' dissatisfiers with teaching as an occupation.

Historical Perspectives

Images of Teachers

The myth and the reality of the historical teacher are far apart in America. There exists a widespread image of teachers past. Popularized in fiction and in warm, if faulty, memories, these teachers were excellent scholars, well respected in their communities, and highly successful in teaching reading, writing, and arithmetic as well as advanced learning to generations of grateful youngsters. Such teachers surely existed, but to say they were uncommon in American history is an understatement—they were the exceptions, not the norm. Nevertheless, this idealized image is often used as a weapon with which to threaten or punish contemporary teachers. If teachers in the past were learned, why are present-day teachers so ill educated? Perhaps, answer the critics, it is because of the anti-intellectualism of schools of education. If teachers in the past were so well respected, why do present-day teachers suffer from a lack of community respect? Perhaps it is because today's teachers are less dedicated, without a sense of calling, and because of the lower moral standards of our contemporary society that allow undesirables to become teachers. If teachers in the past were able to teach most all children to read, spell, and recite the multiplication tables and to know the dates of the Civil War and who wrote *King Lear*, what is wrong with teachers today who fail so miserably in teaching basic skills or cultural literacy? Perhaps it is because today's teachers spend their time in frivolous activities rather than teaching what is important. While I was writing this chapter, I attended a national meeting of educational historians. During the conference, Donald Warren, one of America's best-known historians of the teaching profession and editor of *American Teachers: Histories of a Profession at Work*, was asked why teachers today are not as able as they once were. He replied, correctly I think, to the incredulous questioner that today's teachers are the best we have ever had. I suspect that most historians of teachers would agree. Consider how much difference it might make in popular opinion, and even in the minds of teachers, if we understood that teachers are better educated and more able than they have ever been.

Lortie's "shadowed social standing" has been true of teachers throughout American history. The historical status of teaching has generally been low, and many teachers have been ashamed of their profession. John L. Rury, a historian of the social characteristics of teachers, writes that throughout their history, "teachers have been relegated to the very edge of professional respectability."[14] Over fifty years ago, Willard S. Elsbree wrote the most comprehensive history of the profession, *The American Teacher: Evolution of a Profession in a Democracy*. He found many images of the colonial schoolmaster:

> He was a God-fearing clergyman, he was an unmitigated rogue; he was amply paid, he was accorded a bare pittance; he was a classical scholar, he was all but illiterate; he was licensed by bishop or colonial governor, he was certified only by his own pretensions; he was a cultured gentleman, he was a crude-mannered yokel; he ranked with the cream of society, he was regarded as a menial.[15]

You noticed that the only thing we really learned about colonial school teachers from this quote is that they were male. Women did not become school teachers in large numbers until the mid-nineteenth century, a topic I will explore in some detail in the next chapter. Actually, Elsbree makes more explicit generalizations about colonial schoolmasters than the quote suggests. Giving due allowances for geographical differences (Elsbree, like American historians generally, had a New England bias) and for differences in the type of school (Latin grammar masters had higher status than those who taught in lower schools), he found that colonial schoolmasters had a "rather lowly position," although a graduate of Harvard or Yale had relatively high social status, "probably by virtue of his superior education rather than because of his vocation."[16]

In his more recent study, Rury adds to our understanding of the colonial schoolmaster. He reminds us that in the colonial period most children did not go to school; it was too expensive. The more affluent who did go "undoubtedly expected teachers to represent a social background and value system similar to their own."[17] (As more and more children went to school, the social status of teachers tended to fall.) How, you are asking yourself, could the colonists afford to pay this rather elite group of young men who might be Harvard or Yale graduates? The answer is that school teaching was not looked on as a life-long profession or even a principal calling. During the colonial period, 40 percent of the graduates of Harvard taught, at least for a while. Therefore, teaching was a way for new college graduates to earn their daily bread while waiting for better career opportunities. In the study of one probably typical New England town, it was found that half of the teachers taught for a year or less, "and that none stayed for more than five years."[18] In the South and West, teachers were at least as transient, sometimes teaching in several communities a year. There were, of course, exceptions to these generalizations about roving teachers with short careers. New England's most famous schoolmaster was Ezekiel Cheever who taught Latin in Boston for thirty-eight of his seventy-year teaching career. (You may feel some relief in knowing that the retirement plans in all states now require less time in service.)

The less prestigious town schools and (later) district schools where students were taught to read English often had a school term of only a month or a few weeks a year. And the teachers had status and schooling far below that of the Harvard graduates who taught in the Latin schools. Teaching here was clearly part-time work supplementing other ways of earning a living. Particularly outside of New England, some of the teachers of younger children were indentured servants released from British jails where they had been serving time (usually for petty reasons) if they would emigrate to America. Others were immigrant teachers "bought" off the boat through advertisements such as one in a Baltimore newspaper for "various Irish products" including "school masters, beef, pork, and potatoes."[19] If these teachers were indentured servants, classified newspaper advertisements such as the following might appear: "Ran away: a Servant man who followed the occupation of a Schoolmaster, much given to drinking and gambling."[20]

As early as the colonial period, you may see some of the characteristics of the American teachers that continue throughout their history until the present: (a) an ambiguous status (remember that one of the dissatisfiers of contemporary teachers is a perceived lack of respect for their profession), (b) an occupation to which teachers do not or cannot give full-time attention (some studies indicate that as many as one-half of public school teachers moonlight), and (c) relatively short careers as teachers (the average career of an American public school teacher is seven years).

One of the enduring myths is that the historical teacher was morally superior to contemporary teachers and thus worthy of greater community respect. Surely if such a generalization is true at all it should be true of colonial teachers, particularly in New England where the religious purposes of schooling were so strong. In his classic history of the profession, Elsbree tended to be somewhat protective of the image of teachers: "The colonial schoolmaster was at least as 'good' as his contemporaries and probably better." Yet he found many instances of public attention directed to teachers' drunkenness. He admitted that "overindulgence in alcoholic beverages appears to have been a not uncommon failing of the early schoolmasters." Among other teachers that Elsbree describes, there were the cases of Van Marken of Flatbush who paid "more attention to the tavern than to the school"; of Michael Siperus, "a good for nothing person" who drank and engaged in other "shameful" activities; and of Luther Martin who was "reputed to have spent most of his time in drinking."[21]

You may think I overemphasize the issue of drinking among historical teachers. My purpose is not to defame them but to counteract common myths of yesterday's good teachers with today's unprincipled ones. These myths of highly moral teachers in the past are not only historically incorrect but are damaging to the status of contemporary teachers. In my study of midwestern frontier schools, I found that teacher drinking and drunkenness was considered a common problem.[22] School board members complained that teachers brought their whiskey to school and too many preferred "booze" to teaching. One teacher in frontier Illinois made frequent trips throughout the school day to a sycamore tree in which he hid his bottle. After he punished some students, they complained to the school board about their teacher's drinking. This teacher was popular in the community, and, rather than firing him, the school board passed the following resolution:

> We the directors of Dist. No. ___ find you guilty of drinking whisky while on duty and restrict your indulgence to one small drink at each recess and two at the noon hour, and that you are to take no vengeance on the scholars that appeared as witnesses against you.[23]

Some teachers also became a source of alcohol for students. In his memoirs, one former student told of a teacher who shared his cherry-bounce (a mixture of whiskey and honey) with his students. Many became so "orful sick" that they were not sober enough to walk home, some passing out along the way. Angry parents were able to have the teacher fired.[24]

The image of the nineteenth-century American teacher as a model of virtue, civility, and learning is in conflict with the historical record. The drinking teacher is only one example of nineteenth-century perceptions of teachers much at odds with our present-day polished image of them. Teachers today rightly resent a too-common perception: "Those who can, do; those who can't, teach." More disturbing for your professor, I suspect some add, "Those who can't teach, teach others to teach."

Unfortunately, in the nineteenth century the observation was literally true, particularly in the West and South. One of the early historians of education in Ohio asserted that teaching was regarded as a kind of pension, necessary because county infirmaries (poor houses) were not available. He further complained that schools "were taught by crippled, worn-out old men and women physically unable to scotch hemp and spin flax, and constitutionally opposed to exercise."[25]

A number of contemporary accounts of nineteenth-century teachers indicated that they had physical disabilities of one kind or another and were unable to do physical labor. In what may be an apocryphal story, and from today's perspective an insensitive one, D. D. Banta described the teachers in his Indiana home county as the "one-legged teacher, the lame teacher, the teacher who had fits, the teacher who had been educated for the ministry but owing to his habits of hard drink, had turned to pedagogue, and the teacher who got drunk on Saturday and whipped the entire class on Monday."[26] A group of Kansas settlers debated the qualifications of teaching candidates and finally decided to hire a man with a bad heart because he was unable to do manual labor.[27] Hiring the disabled as teachers because of their inability to earn a living in other ways has a long tradition in America. Elsbree indicates that it was sometimes a policy in colonial America, illustrating the point with the example of the baker who was appointed schoolmaster because "he was impotent in his hand."[28]

Like the colonial teachers described before, teachers of a later era saw teaching as a temporary expedient and remained in any one teaching position for only a short time. Many of the early teachers seem to share the restlessness that was considered characteristic of Americans. In his memoirs of the Indiana frontier, Oliver Johnson remembered that teachers were not men looking for a place to settle down and make a reputation, but "they was more of a rovin class."[29] In his recollections of teachers in the same state, Banta referred to them as a variety of tramps and homeless fellows who traveled around looking for a job.[30] One such person, claiming to be a Methodist minister as well as a teacher, appeared one day from "somewhere," taught for a while, and then mysteriously disappeared to "somewhere."[31]

Persons unfamiliar with the history of teaching in American history are often surprised to discover the remarkably short tenure of teachers in the lower schools. For many young Americans in the nineteenth and early twentieth centuries, school teaching was roughly equivalent to working in fast food today, a way of earning a little money while deciding what to do with their lives. The National Education Association reported that in the 1922-23 school year, the national teacher turnover was 16 percent, with a high of 47 percent in Wyoming.[32] A 1920 survey found that the median tenure of rural school teachers in the United States was two years.[33]

Wayne E. Fuller, in his recent study of country teachers, notes that they were not "career-oriented," rarely staying more than one year in a school. And, like the colonial teachers before them, they rarely remained in teaching for very long. As late as the World War I period, he found that "the average country teacher in Nebraska taught less than two years, and in Pennsylvania less than four." He indicates that only southern teachers appeared to stay in the occupation longer.[34] However, studies of southern rural schools suggests that the tenure of teachers was short there as well. Lawrence Alexander Sharp surveyed 733 rural white teachers in fifteen southern states in 1918 and 1919. Among other questions, he asked them how long they had been in their present positions. Over 60 percent reported they were in their first year, nearly 20 percent were in their second year, and less than 4 percent had taught in their school for five years or more.[35] In 1923 in Union County, Tennessee, the average time that teachers had held their teaching position was less than six months. There were twelve categories of schools studied in Union County, and only one (three-teacher schools) had teachers who had served for an average of at least a year.[36] For persons with such a short time in an occupation, professional status is not possible.

Contemporary teachers are often compared unfavorably with those in the past on the basis of their scholarship. The image of teachers past is that of a paragon of learning, respected throughout the countryside for knowledge of things ancient and modern. This image is frequently used by critics of teachers present to berate contemporary teachers and to explain their lack of respect and pay. There have always been exceptional scholars among teachers of school children. As indicated before, in the colonial period some New England towns almost always hired university graduates as teachers in the Latin grammar schools, and with the feminization of teaching in the mid-nineteenth century, women of high scholarly attainments who were not allowed to use their learning in other occupations taught in the common schools. But every generation of Americans has been critical of the scholarship of most of its teachers, and our contemporary teachers are the best educated in our history.

In colonial America the only scholarly qualification for schoolmasters, particularly of those who taught younger children, was that they be able to read and write, and they often barely met that qualification. The academic credentials of teachers in the nineteenth century were often severely limited. In his memoirs, John Mason Peck, traveling in Missouri and Illinois, complained that "not a few drunken, profane, worthless Irishmen (Peck was anti-Catholic) were perambulating the country, and getting up schools; and yet they could neither speak, read, pronounce, spell or write the English language."[37] Teachers were often hired, not because they were learned, but because they might be able to maintain discipline. "Ignorant strapping" bullies were hired to keep rowdy students "in a state of subdued sulkiness."[38] An example is this interview between the chairman of a local school board and an applicant for a teaching job in New England in the 1860s:

Chairman: How old are you?
Candidate: I was eighteen years old the 27th day of last May.

Chairman:	Where did you last attend school?
Candidate:	At the Academy of S.
Chairman:	Do you think you can make our big youngsters mind?
Candidate:	Yes, I think I can.
Chairman:	Well, I am satisfied. I guess you will do for our school. I will send over the certificate by the children tomorrow.[39]

Criticisms of the ignorance of teachers rivaled any that we have today. In 1856, the school examiner of Monroe County, Indiana, complained that, "We have teachers in our own county that don't know whether we live north or south of the equator, or whether the world turns to the east or west."[40] One teacher who was being interviewed for a job in Des Moines in 1851 was asked his "feelings" about fractions. He responded that "he did not believe in them, and if he could have his way, they would be taken out of arithmetics." It is a commentary on the academic quality of teaching at the time that he was the best applicant and got the job.[41]

Even when boards of education made attempts to examine candidates rigorously, the results were sometimes ludicrous. Occasionally the examiners were unable to answer the very questions they asked. A teaching applicant in Indiana was asked: "What is the product of 25 cents by 25 cents?" The candidate said he didn't know, and "The examiner appeared a bit perplexed and said he thought the answer was six and one fourth cents but he wasn't sure."[42] Sometimes local school boards made up examinations to which no one could know the answers. Here is one in geography:

1. Name all the rivers of the globe.
2. Name all the bays, gulfs, seas, lakes, and other bodies of water on the globe.
3. Name all the cities of the world.
4. Name all the countries of the world.
5. Bound each of the states in the United States.

The candidates were given one hour to complete the examination, and, according to a teacher who took the test, all of the applicants scored 60 percent, even though they were all working on different questions when time was called.[43]

In the next chapter I will review the history of teacher education. It suffices to say for now that the academic quality of most teachers remained low well into the twentieth century.

Dissatisfiers with Teaching

In the introduction to this chapter, I reviewed major satisfiers and dissatisfiers of teachers. The quality of persons entering the profession, particularly before the feminization of teaching, is in part a reflection of the dissatisfiers of teaching as a career. Until the last few generations, most teachers taught in rural district schools where the pay was often so low that teachers could not afford to buy food and rent a place of their own. They were often required to "board around," living a few days or weeks in the home of a student before moving on to another; as an example, more than 70 percent of Nebraska's teachers were still boarding around in 1915.[44] Parents were often poor, and living conditions were sometimes dreadful. In earlier periods homes where teachers boarded were often log cabins—cold in winter, stifling in summer, offering virtually no privacy. One of the satisfiers of teaching today is that you can leave the students at the end of the school day. When teachers boarded around, that was impossible. "Usually there were children in the home who could not be ignored," and, if this were not bad enough, Fuller recounts the bad news that frequently teachers "were forced to share a bed with one of them."[45] The document, "Boarding 'Round in Vermont," is part of American educational folklore. The story may be apocryphal, but the pitfalls of boarding around were real to generations of teachers.

Monday. Went to board at Mr. B's; had a baked gander for dinner; suppose from its size, thickness of the skin and other venerable appearances it must have been one of the first settlers of Vermont; made a slight impression on the patriarch's breast. Supper—cold gander and potatoes. Family consists of the man, good wife, daughter Peggy, four boys, Pompey the dog, and a brace of cats. Fire built in the square room about nine o'clock, and a pile of wood lay by the fireplace; saw Peggy scratch her fingers, and couldn't take the hint; felt squeamish about the stomach, and talked of going to bed; Peggy looked sullen, and put out the fire in the square room; went to bed, and dreamed of having eaten a quantity of stone wall.

Tuesday. Cold gander for breakfast, swamp tea and nut cake–the latter some consolation. Dinner–the legs, &c., of the gander, done up warm–one nearly despatched. Supper–the other leg, &c., cold; went to bed as Peggy was carrying in the fire to the square room; dreamed I was a mud turtle, and got on my back and could not get over again.

Wednesday. Cold gander for breakfast; complained of sickness, and could eat nothing. Dinner–wings, &c., of the gander warmed up; did my best to destroy them, for fear they should be left for supper; did not succeed; dreaded supper all afternoon. Supper–hot Johnny cake; felt greatly revived; thought I had got clear of the gander, and went to bed for a good night's rest; disappointed; very cool night, and couldn't keep warm; got up and stopped the broken window with my coat vest; no use; froze the tip of my nose and one ear before morning.

Thursday. Cold gander again; much discouraged to see the gander not half gone; went visiting for dinner and supper; slept abroad and had pleasant dreams.

Friday. Breakfast abroad. Dinner at Mr. B's; cold gander and potatoes–the latter very good; ate them, and went to school quite contented. Supper–cold gander and no potatoes, bread heavy and dry; had the headache and couldn't eat. Peggy much concerned; had a fire built in the square room, and thought she and I had better sit there out of the noise; went to bed early; Peggy thought too much sleep bad for the headache.

Saturday. Cold gander and hot Indian Johnny cake; did very well. Dinner–cold gander again; didn't keep school this afternoon; weighed and found I had lost six pounds the last week; grew alarmed; had a talk with Mr. B. and concluded I had boarded out his share.

A major dissatisfier of teaching in the past, and in the present, is the teacher workplace: the classroom or the school building. Clifton Johnson offers a colorful description of Connecticut schools in the 1840s:

> Some of the rooms were less than seven feet high; often they had broken windows, clapboards hanging loose, props up at the blinds to keep them in place, stoves without doors, leaky roofs, patches of plaster missing and the rest of the plastering much marred and begrimed; crevices in the floor admitted any quantity of cold air, while the woodwork of the desks and walls was cut and marked "with all sorts of images, some of which would make heathens blush."[46]

This New England school would have been envied by many rural teachers in the South where abandoned cabins, barns, and other outbuildings were used for schools. I know of one case in which school was held in an abandoned smokehouse. As usual, then and now, school facilities for black children were worse. So strong was the prejudice against black public schools in the South following the Civil War that black teachers were sometimes not provided with schools at all: they had to provide their own. They "taught in churches, lodge halls, tenant houses, barns, or whatever abandoned buildings were available."[47] Progress for black schools in the South was excruciatingly slow. As late as 1912, a South Carolina school supervisor wrote that "frequently the county superintendent does not know where they are located, and sometimes the district board cannot tell where the Negro [sic] school is taught."[48]

Americans tend to distort history by romanticizing it. Making the past better than it was also distorts the present by making it worse than it is by comparison. Perhaps nowhere is this phenomenon more pervasive than in our sentimental love affair with the little red schoolhouse (although it was usually white if it was painted at all). As these descriptions of rural schools indicate, they were often very unsatisfactory places for teachers. For the sake of realism and at the risk of being indecorous, I should let you know that a major problem of rural teachers was the outdoor privies. "Squalid and graffiti-covered, they were a challenge to every country teacher who worried about sanitation or decorum."[49] Southern teachers might count themselves lucky if they had privies at all. Even in the early years of the twentieth century, the best many southern rural teachers could do was to direct the girls into the woods in one direction and the boys in another.

Although rural schoolhouses were the workplace of most teachers in the 1800s, by the turn of the century the "new immigration" from southern and eastern Europe and migration of Americans from rural areas were creating new workplaces for an increasing number of teachers: inner-city schools. In 1903-1904, teacher and writer Adele Marie Shaw presented a "dismal portrait" of New York City schools, including "unspeakably unsanitary conditions" where as many as sixty-five unbathed children (for the tenement houses of the time lacked bathrooms) were packed into classrooms built for twenty. Shaw described one gloomy school building which backed up on the water closets or privies of tenements:

> Because of the stench that had floated in the windows, complaint had been made of the yard closets, and I was told that they had been closed and the air purified. I was not conscious of any unpleasant odor, but the closets were not entirely out of use. . . . In this building, which was not atypical, Shaw described the playground as a "small dark basement" in which as many at 500 children were supposed to play: On rainy days they are often crowded so close in the hopeless darkness of the basement that there is barely standing-room. The teacher in charge of the playground must stay in this cell, though to see what is going on was impossible, and although on winter days the place is miserably cold."[50]

Conclusion

In presenting this sometimes unattractive picture of past teachers, I have run the risk of having some of you think that I am too critical of or too negative about teachers, perhaps even wanting to discourage you from a career in teaching. This is not at all true. I spent a number of challenging and satisfying years as a public school teacher, and, like many teachers, teaching is a traditional occupation in my family. Instead, I had two objectives for this critical examination: first, to show the inaccuracy of overly sentimental portraits of teachers in the past which can be used to make insidious comparisons with present teachers and second, to provide some understandings of the historical reasons for the traditionally lowly status of American public school teachers.

The theme of this chapter is that there is nothing new about the lack of respect that American teachers experience. They have long had bad press. Contrary to contemporary myths about teachers in the past, there is much continuity in their low status. Their lack of prestige has resulted from a pervasive perception that many men teachers lacked both elevated moral character and high scholarly attainments.

Throughout American history, teachers have also been dissatisfied with their jobs, and their working conditions have often been intolerable. The result has been that, in the past, teaching has seldom been able to attract and retain the brightest and best of men. But there are also women. In a patriarchal society, entry of women into teaching has had profound effects on this occupation.

Their story and the historical struggle to improve the position of teachers in American society are the subjects of the next essay. Chapter three will demonstrate that I am an optimist rather than a cynic about the possibilities of teachers as agents in improving their own profession.

Notes

1 Dan C. Lortie, *Schoolteacher: A Sociological Study* (Chicago: The University of Chicago Press, 1975).

2 Carnegie Forum on Education and the Economy, *A Nation Prepared: Teachers for the 21st Century*, The Report of the Task Force on Teaching as a Profession: Carnegie Foundation, 1986.

3 John I. Goodlad, *A Place Called School: Prospects for the Future* (New York: McGraw-Hill, 1984), p. 172.

4 Louis Harris and Associates, *Metropolitan Life Survey of the American Teacher* (New York: Metropolitan Life and Affiliated Companies, 1985); Susan J. Rosenholtz, Otto C. Bassler, and Kathleen V. Shoover-Dempsey, "Why Teachers Quit," *Tennessee Teachers*, 53 (March, 1986).

5 Carnegie Forum on Education and the Economy, p. 60.

6 Lortie, p. 10.

7 *Life*, 38 (October 16, 1950).

8 Joseph Mayer Rice, "The Public Schools of St. Louis and Indianapolis," *The Forum*, 15 (December, 1892), p. 430.

9 Goodlad, pp. 186-187.

10 Arthur G. Powell, Eleanor Farrar, and David K. Cohen, *The Shopping Mall High School: Winners and Losers in the Educational Marketplace*, quoted in Carnegie Forum on Education and the Economy, p. 40.

11 *Tomorrow's Teachers: A Report of the Holmes Group* (East Lansing, MI: The Holmes Group, 1986) p. 7.

12 Carnegie Forum on Education and the Economy, p. 60.

13 Gerald Grant, *The World We Created at Hamilton High* (Cambridge: Harvard University Press, 1988), p. 141.

14 John L. Rury, "Who Became Teachers?: The Social Characteristics of Teachers in American History," *American Teachers: Histories of a Profession at Work*, ed. Donald Warren (New York: Macmillan Co., 1989), p. 11.

15 Willard S. Elsbree, *The American Teacher: Evolution of a Profession in a Democracy* (New York: American Book Company, 1939), p. 123.

16 *Ibid.*, pp. 116, 121.

17 Rury, p. 12.

18 *Ibid.*, p. 14.

19 Michael W. Sedlak, "Let Us Go and Buy a School Master: Historical Perspectives on the Hiring of Teachers in the United States, 1750-1980," *American Teachers: Histories of a Profession at Work*, ed. Donald Warren (New York: Macmillan Co., 1989), p. 259.

20 Clifton Johnson, *Old-Time Schools and School-books* (New York: Dover Publications, 1962 [1904]), p. 33.

21 Elsbree, pp. 18-19.

22 Clinton B. Allison, "The Feminization of Teaching Revisited: The Case of the Ne're-Do-Well Man Teacher," *The Socio-Cultural Foundations of Education and the Evolution of Education Policies in the United States*, ed. James J. Van Patten (Lewiston, NY: The Edwin Mellon Press, 1991).

23 C. C. Carter, "Frontier Sketches: The Schoolmaster," *Journal of the Illinois State Historical Society*, 32 (June, 1939), p. 228.

24 Rufus Babcock (ed.), *Forty Years of Pioneer Life: Memoir of John Mason Peck, D.D.* (Philadelphia: American Baptist Publication Society, 1864, reprinted by Southern Illinois University Press, 1965), p. 124.

25 James J. Burns, *Educational History of Ohio* (Columbus: Historical Publishing Co., 1905), p. 21.

26 D. D. Banta, "The Early Schools of Indiana," *Indiana Magazine of History*, 2 (1906), p. 85.

27 Lloyd C. Smith, "A Historical Outline of the Territorial Common Schools in the State of Kansas," *Bulletin of Information, Studies in Education Number 24*, Kansas State Teachers College of Emporia (Emporia, 1942), pp. 25-26.

28 Elsbree, p. 34.

29 "A Home in the Woods: Oliver Johnson's Reminiscences of Early Marion County," *Indiana Historical Publications*, 16 (1951), p. 175.

30 Banta, p. 85.

31 Elbert Waller, "Some Half-Forgotten Towns in Illinois," *Transactions of the Illinois State Historical Society*, 34 (1927), 73.

32 Cited in Irving P. Foote, *Tenure of High School Teachers in Louisiana* (Contribution to Education No. 93, George Peabody College for Teachers, 1931), p. 12.

33 *Ibid.*, p. 7.

34 Wayne E. Fuller, "The Teacher in the Country School," *American Teachers: Histories of a Profession at Work*, ed. Donald Warren (New York: Macmillan Co., 1989).

35 Lawrence Alexander Sharp, *The Present Status of Rural Teachers in the South* (Contributions to Education Number Two, George Peabody College for Teachers, undated, data collected in 1918-19).

36 Clinton B. Allison, "The Country Life Movement in Tennessee: Educationists and Rural Reform," Paper presented at *History of Education Society* (Atlanta, November, 1985).

37 Babcock, p. 123.

38 Ruben Gold Thwaites, *Historical Sketch of the Public Schools of Madison, Wisconsin* (Madison: M. J. Cantwell Book and Job Printer, 1886), p. 13.

39 Elsbree, pp. 181-182.

40 James Albert Woodburn, "James Woodburn: Hoosier Schoolmaster," *Indiana Magazine of History*, 32 (September, 1936), pp. 235-236.

41 John A. Nash, "A Selection from the Autobiography of John A. Nash," *The Iowa Journal of History and Politics*, 13 (April, 1915), p. 201.

42 Elsbree, p. 183.

43 Sedlak, pp. 261-262.

44 Fuller, p. 111.

45 *Ibid.*

46 Clifton Johnson, p. 133.

47 Fuller, p. 101.

48 *Ibid.*, p. 103.

49 *Ibid.*, p. 112.

50 Adele Marie Shaw, "The True Character of the New York Public Schools," *The World's Work*, VII (December, 1903). Reproduced in Nancy Hoffman, *Woman's True Profession: Voices from the History of Teaching* (Old Westbury, NY: The Feminist Press, 1981), pp. 218-227.

III

Women Teachers and the Struggle for Occupational Justice: Is Feminism An Answer?

In addition to the dissatisfiers of teachers discussed in chapter two, there is pay. Teaching is an underpaid profession; teachers have always been underpaid, and Americans have always had better teachers than they have paid for. Whereas teaching in the nineteenth century was often considered a part-time and temporary position—not a real job for a real man, it often represented a career opportunity for well-educated and intellectually able women who, because of the gender prejudice in society, were unable to find other suitable work. A lack of economic justice for women has had significant consequences for teaching careers: it has brought into teaching many of the occupation's most academically talented persons and, in a gender-biased society, it has created a justification for low salaries. As the women's movement has strengthened, feminist teachers have also provided powerful agents in the struggle to improve teaching as a career.

Susan B. Carter has recently written a history of teacher pay. She points out that since 1900, male teachers have earned only a fraction of the salaries of other college graduates. For example, in 1930, male teachers were paid 60 percent of what civil engineers earned. In 1985, their salary was only 57 percent of what civil engineers were paid. She compared teachers' salaries not only to other white-collar workers but also to the wages of manufacturing workers as well. Over the past century there have been fluctuations in the income of teachers compared to these others—generally stable until the 1920s, some overall improvement from 1929 to 1970, a drop in the 1970s and early 1980s, and some recent improvement.[1]

Some critics of teachers, particularly among neo-conservatives, complain that over the last decade or so the salaries of teachers have increased dramatically without a corresponding rise in standardized test scores. "If you want to improve schools, don't put more money down that rat hole of teacher pay," they say. Leaving aside for the moment the thorny, politically-loaded issues of standardized test scores as proof of teacher effectiveness or even of "learning," the "increase" in teachers' salaries is deceptive. Much of the salary increase took place during a period of inflation when the value of dollars decreased. During this time, the salaries of other college graduates were increasing as well, leaving teachers relatively little better off. Carter concludes that, compared to other fields, as recently as 1985 teachers' salaries were still below what they had been in 1975.[2]

With teachers' salaries lower than those of other professions and occupations, how have generations of Americans found enough teachers to "keep school"? Ironically, part of the answer is found in gender (and racial) prejudice. When employment opportunities were limited because of discrimination, salaries too low to appeal to educated men looked attractive to many women. An issue that our generation is having to face relates to what happens to the quality of the teaching profession when talented and well-educated women (and African-Americans) have increased career opportunities other than teaching.

Historical Perspectives

The Feminization of Teaching

In chapter two, I write about teachers as if they were primarily men, and they were until the mid-nineteenth century. Reflecting on his school days in the 1820s and 1830s, Oliver Johnson of Indiana wrote that teaching "wasn't a woman's job, any more than milkin a cow was a man's job." And he added in a comment that reflected the prejudices of generations of Americans that "then agin it took purty much of a man to handle the big boys and girls."[3]

By the time of the Civil War, a majority of public school teachers were women; by 1900 about 70 percent were women, and the ratio has remained fairly constant since. In American history, no other development in public schools has been as significant as has this change in the gender of teachers. How do we explain such a revolutionary change? Why were women rather than men hired in increasing numbers at mid-nineteenth century? Was it because women could be paid less or because they were considered better teachers of youth? The feminization of teaching had multi-causes: economic, social, and ideological. Among the causes were changes in the labor market that made teaching less attractive to men; increasing demands for teachers as a consequence of the successes of the common school movement; changing perception about proper or, at least, acceptable roles for women; and changing purposes for public schools. In an influential study for the National Institute of Education, Myra H. Strober and David B. Tyack conclude that feminization of teaching was largely a result of functions of the labor market and the formalization of schooling.[4]

First, I will look at the relationship between the common school movement (what Strober and Tyack mean by the formalization of schooling) and the feminization of teaching. As indicated in chapter one, the common school movement in the mid-nineteenth century was a wide-spread attempt to solve social problems through the schools. The major purpose of schooling was moral and character education.

The emphasis was on the social purposes of schools. Common schools were to teach a set of common values—a Protestant, industrial ethic aimed at Americanizing immigrant children and socializing country children whose families were being lured to the cities by promises of prosperity. The common school leaders worried about the breakdown of the family in cities. Public schools were to be surrogate families for the schoolchild. Feminization of teaching was, in part, a consequence of this "ideology of domesticity." In the conventional wisdom of the nineteenth century, women were considered to be morally and spiritually superior (and intellectually inferior) to men. In light of the goals of the common school, it was "not only justified but made imperative" that they enter schools as "surrogate mothers." The school, according to Michael B. Katz, "was to resemble a home . . . presided over by a wise and loving mother."[5] The moral problems of crime and poverty were to be corrected by providing each delinquent child with a wise, morally superior mother, a middle-class teacher—a "republican mother." In an often quoted remark, common school leader Henry Barnard proclaimed in 1840: "Heaven has plainly appointed females as the natural instructors of young children, and endowed them with those qualities of mind and disposition, which pre-eminently fit them for such a task."[6]

One of the promises of these nineteenth-century school reformers was that women teachers, with their perceived natural nurturing instincts, would be able to discipline without the harshness, even cruelty, of many schoolmasters. The reformers, historian Jo Anne Preston writes, claimed that women's positive feelings for children, as well as their superior morals, enabled female teachers to govern their students by "the silken bond of affection" and "moral suasion."[7]

In chapter two, I examine perceptions of male teachers as often ne'er-do-wells: unlettered or barely literate, emotionally unstable, cruel, or drinkers. They must have been thought incapable of furthering the school reformers' goals of social control, by putting or keeping children on the narrow path of nineteenth-century evangelical Protestantism. The work of common school promoters in convincing popular opinion that teaching was women's "true profession" was surely made easier by images of the ne'er-do-well male teacher.[8]

The nineteenth-century perception of the nature of women was a product of a patriarchal society, and the images of women that resulted served the interests of men. Jo Anne Preston (among other feminist historians) argues that the women of that era were much different from the images of them promulgated by male school reformers. Women teachers "wanted to achieve economic independence and to continue their scholarly pursuits. . . . They expressed little interest in mothering the children or inculcating them with morals."[9]

For women it was "a period of opportunity and oppression." Feminization of teaching provided work outside the home, but paternalistic treatment by males pervaded both the working lives and the home lives of teachers. Paternalistic treatment of women teachers was, of course, much in keeping with our patriarchal society. Women teachers were supposed to control and manage the children; in turn they were controlled and managed by their male overseers.[10]

The necessity of dividing life and labor into different spheres based on gender was considered just common sense by most Americans until the last few years (and the persistence of this attitude is a major obstacle to advancing teaching as a career). Men were considered to be the natural decision makers and administrators because they were the rational gender. Because women were emotional by nature, they were to be the followers. Because of their socialization, "women teachers assumed positions subservient to their male superiors whom they were to consider as their fathers."[11]

Paternalistic treatment of women teachers was partly a function of their age; they were often quite young. Especially in rural areas, teachers were as young as sixteen years old, and occasionally even younger. In a study of the teachers of Dane County, Wisconsin, in 1860, Martha Coon found that more than 25 percent of the women teachers were eighteen or younger, and more than 80 percent were unmarried and living with their parents.[12] In the one- and two-room schools of the nineteenth and early twentieth centuries, these young women teachers were sought after not only because they could be paid less but also because they were thought to be relatively easy to control by male school boards and other influential men in the community.

Even in the larger, graded schools where both women and men taught, they had different spheres. In a recent study of gender and teaching, Geraldine Joncich Clifford quotes an article written for an influential education journal by a male educator in 1906: "Women are nimble-witted in tact and moral virtues but their store of information is less deep and less thorough."[13] Because such perceptions were widely accepted, it was considered good practice for male teachers to have higher salaries to teach older students and harder subjects.

One consequence of the feminization of teaching was the creation of the modern school principal. It was widely believed that women could not maintain proper discipline, that older boys would always be an unmanageable problem for them, whereas the natural male sphere was administration and policy making. To school leaders the answer was easy and obvious—appoint male overseers of female teachers. The result has been the elementary school you are familiar with—a dozen or so female teachers (with perhaps a male sixth-grade teacher) and a male principal. Historian David Tyack has called this common pattern the pedagogical harem. The results have been deleterious for women and men teachers alike. It has fixed "the subordinate role of the classroom teacher," Carl Kaestle writes, "reinforcing the hierarchical organization desired by professional male educators."[14]

Until well into the twentieth century, the gender and age of teachers allowed local boards of education to control their private as well as their working lives. Paternalistic attitudes towards teachers is evident in the following rules for teachers, allegedly from the 1920s:

Don't get married, and don't keep company with men.
Be home between the hours of 8:00 p.m. and 6:00 a.m.
Don't loiter in ice cream parlors.
Don't smoke cigarettes, and don't drink beer, wine or whiskey.
Don't leave town without permission.
Don't ride in a carriage or automobile with any man except your father or brother.
Don't dress in bright colors, dye your hair or use face powder, mascara, or lipstick, and wear at least two petticoats.

Teachers in a number of states have claimed that before being hired they were asked to sign statements that they would adhere to these rules. The rules may only be a part of our educational folklore, but they reflect common treatment of women teachers in the period.

In order to assure their virtuous behavior, women teachers were often told where they must live. If they did not live at home with their parents, they were sometimes required to live in teachers' dormitories or in teacherages, houses where the principal and his family often lived on the first floor and single teachers had bedrooms upstairs. In schools too small to support teacherages or dormitories, single women teachers were often required to live in a particular boarding house where the older female owner could keep a watchful eye over their manners and morals and could make sure they received a healthy diet and got eight hours of sleep each night.

Women teachers were not only prohibited from marrying; they were often discouraged from dating, and at least one teacher contract required them to promise that they would not fall in love. The policy created deceptions, of course, and the secretly married teacher, full of anxiety about being discovered, was part of the culture of teaching a few generations ago. The prohibition against married women (but not men) teachers was usually justified on the basis that homemaking and school teaching were both full-time jobs, and, if a teacher were married, either her husband and children or her students would suffer from a lack of her full attention and devotion. Teaching jobs were sometimes treated as though they were welfare programs, and there were objections that if a woman who already had a husband to support her took a teaching position, she was depriving someone else of a livelihood. One of the most bizarre (both racist and class-biased) reasons for discouraging married teachers is found in a 1931 journal for school administrators:

> My chief objection to married women teaching is the fact that it leads almost necessarily to childless homes or to the restriction of children in homes that really should produce more children. Every time you elect a married teacher, you tacitly endorse and encourage such practices which are the most reprehensible sins of the upper and middle classes.[15]

There are other, if usually unstated, reasons that school administrators and boards of education wanted young single women teachers. Again, young unmarried teachers were thought to be easier to govern; in an institution controlled by older men, young women would have little choice but to do as they were told in regard to curriculum, teaching methods, and treatment of students. In addition, I suspect that school leaders, consciously or unconsciously, were often looking for secular nuns. Character development–the teaching of proper values–was a major goal of the school; and pure young women, unsullied by sex and marriage, were preferred instructors of virtue.

The prohibition against married women as teachers was weakened during World War I when tens of thousands of men teachers were drafted and women took their places. In many cases these often mature women proved to be exceptionally able and popular teachers, and boards of education faced parental protests when they attempted to enforce pre-war policies by firing them. Sometimes married women who were already teaching were allowed to keep their jobs, but the old rules were enforced in hiring new teachers. World War II virtually destroyed the prohibition. Because of the shortage of workers of all kinds, many more women went into the labor market, including teaching. Following the war, changing job opportunities and the baby boom made a return to the old, already anachronistic policy impossible. Pay differentials between the genders continued for some time, however. When I started my public teaching career back so long ago that the earth was still cooling (actually in 1958), I was paid $200 more a year simply because I was a man.

Dee Ann Spencer analyzes three generations of women teachers. The first she calls contractual singlehood when, as I have been describing, women teachers' lives were circumscribed by all sorts of rules and regulations created by men in a patriarchal society, including prohibitions against marriage. Usually the teacher had only herself to support. The second generation, during the 1950s, she labeled teaching as insurance. Married teachers provided a second income for extras and as insurance if "something happened to their husbands," the chief breadwinner. We are now in the third generation where the income of women teachers is seldom optional. Two incomes to support a family are now the norm if a middle-class lifestyle is to be maintained. And many women teachers are heads of families with children to support. Their salaries are no longer just "insurance" or for luxuries but for a living.[16]

Teacher Activism

Teachers have not just been victims of their history. They have also been active agents in changing their profession as their control over their professional lives has increased over time. Historian Wayne Urban has related this history in *Why Teachers Organized* and other publications.[17] In the eighteenth and nineteenth centuries, teachers possessed little power or even influence over their conditions. Schools belonged to the community, and teachers were often considered merely hired hands. About the only recourse a teacher had when their situation became unbearable was to move to another school or to quit teaching.

Conditions did not improve with the success of the common school movement. The centralization and bureaucratization that accompanied the common schools changed the relationship between teachers and their employers by creating occupational hierarchies that put teachers in subordinate positions. Attempts by teachers to gain control over their professional practice or to improve their pay or working conditions have always been viewed with alarm by both members of the educational hierarchy and by boards of education. Tenure laws did not usually protect teachers until the middle of the twentieth century; teacher "agitators" were simply dismissed.

Early in this century when it appeared that teachers, in large numbers, might organize unions, school administrators developed what was to become a common tactic—developing teachers' organizations which were administratively controlled (in the private sector these organizations are called company unions). Among the first of these were teachers' councils which were supposed to give a voice to teachers. Urban explains their real purpose:

> Superintendents and university professors of educational administration who proposed councils at this time were much more concerned with the creation of vehicles with which they might head off attempts of teachers to organize unions and other associations independent of the local administration, than they were with establishing legitimate channels to represent the teachers' "voice."[18]

But there were always courageous teachers who refused to be controlled by the hierarchy. In 1897, women elementary teachers organized the first successful teachers' union, the Chicago Teachers Federation. They quickly gained members as a result of their successful campaigns to increase salaries; and in 1902, they joined the Chicago affiliate of the American Federation of Labor. A national teachers' union, the American Federation of Teachers (AFT), was formed in 1912. The AFT affiliated with the national labor movement by joining the American Federation of Labor in 1916.[19] Although the AFT got off to a good start, it lost power and influence during the politically conservative 1920s. Much like in the 1980s, the most powerful voices in American society belonged to the industrialists and other business leaders who "branded unions as dangerous, and even un-American."[20] Teachers, many of whom have always been uncomfortable with unions, were unable to resist the powerful forces of business at the time.

The other well-known (and much larger) national teachers' association is the National Education Association (NEA), organized in 1857. Through most of its history, male administrators and college professors dominated the NEA (the original constitution limited membership to "gentlemen"); the voices of teachers, particularly women teachers, were barely heard. Women were allowed to become members of the NEA after the Civil War, and the first woman president of the NEA, Ella Flagg Young, was elected in 1910. Teachers were eventually able to change the NEA constitution to require that women were to become president of the organization every other year, a significant gain for both teachers and women. But since the real administrative power in the NEA was its executive secretary, "a male who had close ties to school administrators," the "victory" over male-administrator domination was less significant than it may seem.[21]

In the militant 1960s, the power of teachers increased in the NEA. Adopting pro-union tactics, teachers supported direct collective bargaining between themselves and boards of education. Although, in deference to the anti-union sentiments and the professional aspirations of many teachers, such bargaining was often called professional negotiations. The best example of the new teacher militancy was a number of teachers' strikes in the 1960s and 1970s (supported by both the NEA and the AFT), although most teachers were and continue to be uncomfortable with strikes. Urban explains why:

> To go on strike was to engage in (usually) illegal activity which graphically contradicted the image of teachers as public servants dedicated to their clients. Strikes also contrasted severely with "professional" ideology of both the national teacher organizations . . . and shocked many segments of the public–and of teachers–outside of the cities in which they took place.[22]

Teachers within the NEA also pushed the organization into more political activity, directly supporting pro-teacher and pro-public schools candidates. State and local NEA affiliates formed local political activity committees to campaign for boards of education members and pro-education governors and state legislatures. The national organization created a political action committee, NEA-PAC. The NEA endorsed a candidate for president for the first time in 1976, Jimmy Carter.

Teachers made many gains in control over their profession in the activist 1960s and early 1970s. That militant period was a time when many of the less powerful groups in American society demanded a higher degree of social justice for themselves. Women were in the vanguard of that movement, and the activism and increased sense of power among them provided leadership among teachers in the struggle to improve their professional lives.

By the 1970s it was clear that classroom teachers had finally gained control of the NEA. The change in leadership was accompanied by a quick exit from the organization by superintendents and principals. They tended to align themselves with boards of education rather than teachers and to consider themselves "management" rather than "labor" in professional negotiations.

Political and social activism generally was condemned by the powerful voices in American society during the conservation 1980s, and that decade was a particularly unfriendly time for teacher activism. The NEA had endorsed the Democratic opponent of the immensely popular President Reagan whose administration was frequently perceived as teacher bashing by educational leaders. As often happens when political and economic leaders do not want to take responsibility for difficulties or when they are unable to create public policy to solve problems, they blame the schools and, by inference, teachers. The recent overwhelming economic problem was, of course, the inability of the American economy to compete successfully with Europe and Japan in the world marketplace. The reasons for this American failure were immensely complicated, but American business and the national administration often took an easy and simplistic way of escaping from their responsibilities for failures: the public schools had failed to produce human capital that was as literate and knowledgeable as the products of foreign schools. Business leaders, with anti-union biases and top-down management styles, were encouraged to take a more active role on commissions studying educational issues. They were joined by education governors, who were also often conservative and business-oriented. They often proposed merit pay or "career ladders" for teachers as a means of improving schools, thereby fostering an inappropriate kind of competition in a teaching culture where teachers are more comfortable and effective with a cooperative, democratic style.

Teacher Education: A Problem and a Solution

You may have experienced condescending behavior from students and perhaps even faculty from other departments when they learned that you are in teacher education. Teacher training has long been looked upon with contempt by some in the university community. According to the folklore of the university, it is a place of Mickey Mouse courses where students of doubtful academic ability receive "A" grades for making hand puppets and preparing bulletin boards. Of course this view of teacher education is a distortion; in reality, teacher education in many universities is becoming one of the most selective of the professional schools and the curriculum is becoming increasingly demanding. But university folklore dies slowly, and enough pap and silliness remains to give critics sufficient anecdotes to keep the legends alive.

Along with teacher unionization and militancy, more demanding teacher education has long been proposed as another way of increasing prestige for teachers. Since the common school movement of the mid-nineteenth century, reformers have argued that professional status depends on high quality professional training. Teaching has been compared to other professions, particularly to the practice of medicine, where tougher selection requirements and more rigorous educational requirements led to higher status and pay, whereas the weak preparation of teachers, low pay, and the kind of paternalistic treatment of teachers discussed before have gone hand-in-hand.

Critics of the academic quality of teacher education programs are omnipresent. A generation ago, in 1963, two popular and influential books were published that were extremely critical of the low academic quality of teacher education: James B. Conant's *The Education of American Teachers* and James D. Koerner's *The Miseducation of American Teachers*. In 1986, Reginald G. Damerell published a self-serving critique: *Education's Smoking Gun: How Teachers Colleges Have Destroyed Education in America*. And, in 1991, Rita Kramer joined the course of boos directed at teacher education with *Ed School Follies: The Miseducation of America's Teachers*.

Although much less bombastic and hypercritical, the two most prestigious contemporary reform reports on teachers and their preparation—*Tomorrow's Teachers: A Report of the Holmes Group* and *A Nation Prepared: Teachers for the Twenty-First Century* (a report of the Carnegie Forum on Education)—also recommend significant academic improvements in the academic preparation of teachers.

The quality of education for teachers was worse in the past. As indicated in chapter two, teachers in the colonial and early national periods were often sadly lacking in formal education; many had only a rudimentary knowledge of reading, writing, and arithmetic. Although college graduates might be found in Latin Grammar Schools, indentured servants and other persons at the lowest levels of society were commonly hired to teach in town and district schools. The formal requirements were few. For example, New England communities required the approval of ministers before one could teach.

The training of teachers explicitly to be teachers was not seriously undertaken until the common school movement of the early nineteenth century, when normal schools were created. If you are at all of a curious nature, you may want to know why a teacher training institution was called a normal school. The answer is that it was an idea imported from France. Victor Cousin, a professor of philosophy in the University of Paris, was commissioned by the French Parliament to develop a teacher training school that was to be the *norm* or standard for such institutions. A Congregational minister, Samuel Hall, may be considered the "father" of teacher education in the United States. He established a teacher-training seminary in Vermont in 1823, and, in 1830, established the normal department at Phillips Andover Academy. The first state normal schools were in Massachusetts; four were established by the legislature in 1838 with the first opening in Lexington in 1839. They quickly spread to other states. New York established a normal school in Albany in 1844.

The leaders of the common school movement supported normal schools enthusiastically. The idea of professionally trained teachers, using up-to-date methods, was central to their educational reforms. It is not surprising that in keeping with their attitudes on the desirability of women teachers, the first state normal school at Lexington was for women only. Others allowed both sexes to enroll, but most normalities were women. By 1875 normal schools were accepted throughout the country, except in the South where they did not become common until the early twentieth century. Normal schools were usually two-year institutions with students entering at age sixteen or seventeen. In the beginning, the curriculum consisted of a review of the elementary school subjects in addition to some art and music, scriptural reading, and lectures on schoolkeeping. Practice teaching was required, often in an attached laboratory school. Normal schools were not scholarly institutions. Historian Jurgen Herbst writes that "Academic requirements were intentionally kept low."[23] Colleges and universities condemned normal schools for their low standards, lack of scholarship, and emphasis on mechanical rules for teaching. In institutions of higher education, the tradition of professors looking on teacher education with suspicion was established very early. As an example, in 1891, when the University of Tennessee established a new Teachers Department, the Board of Trustees and faculty were adamant that the new department was in "no sense a Normal Department":

> Our teachers have already sufficient opportunity for that kind of training, if they want it. The purpose of the University is to advance Knowledge. . . . For the lazy ways, the short courses leading to long degrees, the mechanical methods, and the mere devices in teaching, we have no place here.[24]

As time went on, normal schools came to resemble present-day community colleges rather than just teacher training institutions. They were a place, inexpensive and close to home, where rural youth could continue their schooling. "The normalities were on the move both socially and geographically," Herbst writes, "and few stayed or returned to play the role of county schoolmaster or schoolmistress."[25]

In many places in rural America, particularly in the South, even normal school graduates were rare. Although many teachers had no training at all, some received a few weeks of instruction in summer normal institutes. As an example, such institutes were conducted on the campus of the University of Tennessee from 1880 to 1898. The academic requirements in the one-month institutes were low. Systematic instruction was difficult because of the comings and goings of students and faculty who drifted in and out as they pleased. Students were allowed to enroll even in the last week of the institute, and many who enrolled at the beginning stayed only for a week or two. Examinations were usually optional, but those who took the examination and scored at least 65 percent could have a teaching certificate valid for a year. Those who attended for three summers could have a lifetime certificate.[26]

In the late nineteenth and early twentieth centuries, many teachers were trained in normal classes in high schools where usually only women were allowed to enroll in teacher training classes. In large cities the graduates usually taught in the elementary grades in the same district where they received their training.[27] In some rural areas, particularly in the South, most teachers who received any formal training at all were trained in high schools rather than in normal schools. In Tennessee, as an example, in 1922 there were only twenty-two graduates of normal schools teaching in the 3,500 one-room schools of the state. In contrast, about 300 graduates of the one-year training programs of the forty teacher-training high schools of the state were teaching in these rural schools. The low level of these teacher-training programs may be gauged by the requirements for establishing them in a high school. A separate room for teacher training had to be provided, and the school had to have a "professional library" of at least sixty approved books. The teachers of the normal classes had to be college graduates with at least two years of "successful teaching experience."[28]

In part because high schools were becoming more common in the latter part of the nineteenth century, new teacher education institutions with more rigorous requirements were established. It was the common belief that high school teachers needed higher levels of preparation than elementary teachers. Normal schools often evolved into four-year degree-granting institutions, sometimes called normal universities and many of the state colleges and universities, particularly the land grant institutions, were creating professorships in pedagogy.

The state-wide degree-granting normal universities were to be more prestigious institutions than the old normal schools, and there was a sexist dimension to this search for higher status. The emphasis was on the training of men high school teachers. Herbst presents Illinois Normal University as a prototype. Its leader in the early twentieth century, David Felmley, insisted that professionalism depended on men, and that it was a mistake to limit normal school to the training of elementary teachers who would inevitably be women:

> To Felmley, professionalism meant that only men could be professionals, and therefore women, who would continue to teach in elementary schools, were excluded from the ranks of the profession. He argued that if the normal school succeeded in attracting men students, it would transform education into a profession, and teaching into an esteemed vocation.[29]

Men trained in normal universities would become the administrators, the teachers of the hard subjects (especially the sciences), and they would add "vigor to athletic, oratorical, musical, and dramatic contests."[30]

As indicated above, universities also began to establish professorships of pedagogy: the Universities of Iowa in 1873, Michigan and Wisconsin in 1879, and Indiana and Cornell in 1886. Teacher education invariably led to an increase in women students in universities. The University of Tennessee's new Teachers Department provided a back door for women to enter what had been an all-male institution. In 1891, the year the Department opened, a member of the board of trustees proposed that "lady teachers" be admitted. The faculty agreed, but, in a paternalistic statement, they made it clear that women students would not be coddled, that they should not come to the University to be "polished or finished." The faculty need not have worried; in 1894, women were awarded scholarships as the best students in the freshman, sophomore, and junior classes.[31]

Inevitably competition developed between normal schools and education departments in universities. Normal schools attempted to increase their status by changing their names to teachers colleges; and by 1930, sixty-nine had made this transition. In places as different as Wisconsin and Tennessee, compromises were attempted that limited normal schools or teachers colleges to training elementary teachers, primarily women, while universities would train high school teachers and administrators, mainly men. (The gender bias is again obvious.) The compromises failed to work. As Herbst put it in discussing the Wisconsin experience: The proposal "foundered on the shoals of popular opposition."[32] As indicated before, the populace wanted general education close to home for their youth, and they defeated attempts to limit the role of normal schools to training elementary teachers. After World War II and the flood of students created by the GI Bill, state legislatures often designated normal schools or teacher colleges as regional general purpose universities.

Conclusion

Meliorism for the dissatisfiers of teaching has at least three components: continuing success of the women's movement, activist teachers who continue to support their unions, and reforms in teacher education. The first is the most important. Most public school teachers are women, and both genders have suffered from patriarchal and paternalistic treatment. Low pay and lack of prestige are consequences of an undervaluing of the work of women in our society, and significant improvements are not likely until the status of women is increased. It behooves all teachers, male and female alike, to be feminists.

One of the most counterproductive things that a person interested in the quality of teaching as a career can say is "I am not a feminist, but . . ." with the but usually being followed by what is essentially a feminist position. Of course it is important to remember that there isn't just one way to be a feminist. Feminists speak with many different voices. Through most of the twentieth century in America, feminists have emphasized equal opportunity for women, a position that can be called liberal feminism. Liberal feminists argue that males and females are basically the same and apparent differences result from acculturation, particularly in unequal expectations and opportunities for boys and girls. Liberal feminists strive for equality with men; examples include attempting to assure more opportunities for women in school administration and in the education professoriate and demanding equal pay for women and their male counterparts. A goal of some liberal feminists is to make the schools "gender free." Liberal feminists emphasize the idea of assimilation; men and women should be equally represented and treated the same in all fields.[33]

A more radical, post-modern feminist position is that women are significantly different from men in their intellectual and moral perspectives. The emphasis among these feminists is on women transforming the professions which they enter by bringing their own special qualities, their ways of knowing and being, to their work. The goal of these more radical feminists is not to get women an equal place in a patriarchal system, not to become masculinized, but to keep "their own ways of experiencing and looking at the world."[34]

These transforming or relational (because they put much emphasis on relationships and nurturing) feminists criticize male-dominated schools for their emphasis on abstract thought, competitiveness, assertiveness, objectivity, and hierarchical relationships. According to these feminists, the quality of school life would be enhanced if women educators brought more of their ways of being to schools. More emphasis would be placed on interrelatedness, cooperation, subjectivity, compassion, and most important, the centrality of nurturing.[35] Nel Noddings summarizes some of the changes that would take place with feminist pedagogy:

> a shift from teacher to students as the center of attention; openness and dialogue; student-to-student talk; increased projects; more opportunities for direct contact in the field; variable modes of evaluation; more generous and direct help in learning; and a reluctance to grade on the basis of "natural" talent or test scores.[36]

Certainly, liberal (assimilation) and relational (transformation) do not exhaust the possible feminist positions. Some leftist feminists see relational or transforming feminist as "reclaiming stereotypes" from the nineteenth century when it was widely accepted that women and men were different and women were the natural nurturers. Some critical feminists argue that these gender stereotypes marginalized women then, and may well do so now. These feminists reject the idea that women are nurturers and men are not as more a reflection of ideology than reality: men do nurture, women are competitive.[37] Feminist law professor Joan C. Williams writes that relational feminists "reclaim the compliments of Victorian gender ideology while rejecting its insults."[38]

Union activities are also important in improving teaching as a career. Union/management agreements have raised salaries and can mandate structural changes. Indeed researchers, in a quality of the educational workplace study, found that in school systems with strong union contracts more time was available for professional exchanges and teachers were more satisfied with their workplace.[39]

As a teacher educator, I am convinced that, for teaching as a career to improve, teachers must be empowered and that more rigorous teacher education is central to their empowerment. In part, it is a matter of perception. Teachers need to be perceived as able scholars who have successfully competed with the best in colleges and universities for degrees and have had further rigorous preparation for their profession. And intellectual skills are functional, they empower. Teachers who think, speak, and write well are more articulate champions of their professional workplace. They assault the "reflexive conservatism" that Lortie warned about and that keeps teachers in "their place." They can provide the intellectual power to analyze policy and to effectively participate in policy debates. Higher salaries and professional working conditions depend on a critical mass of persons perceived to be intellectually able, with the resulting sense of self-esteem.

Notes

1 Susan B. Carter, "Incentives and Rewards to Teaching," *American Teachers: Histories of a Profession at Work,* ed. Donald Warren (New York: Macmillan Publishing Co., 1989).

2 *Ibid.*, p. 55.

3 "A Home in the Woods: Oliver Johnson's Reminiscences of Early Marion County," *Indiana Historical Publications*, 16 (1951), p. 55.

4 David B. Tyack and Myra H. Strober, *Women and Men in the Schools: A History of the Sexual Structuring of Educational Employment* (Washington: National Institute of Education, 1981, Grant Number NIE-G-79-0020).

5 Michael B. Katz, "The Origins of Public Education: A Reassessment," *History of Education Quarterly*, 16 (Winter, 1976), p. 89.

6 Jo Anne Preston, "Female Aspiration and Male Ideology: School-teaching in Nineteenth-Century New England," *Current Issues in Women's History*, ed. Arina Angerman et al., (London: Routledge, 1989), p. 175.

7 *Ibid.*, p. 176.

8 Clinton B. Allison, "The Feminization of Teaching Revisited: The Case of the Ne're-Do-Well Man Teacher," *The Socio-Cultural Foundations of Education and the Evolution of Educational Policies in the United States*, ed. James J. Van Patten (Lewiston, NY: The Edwin Mellen Press, 1991).

9 Preston, p. 175.

10 Susan R. Martin, *Women as Teachers: From Feminization to Feminism,* Paper presented at the American Educational Studies Association (Chicago, 1989), p. 13.

11 *Ibid.*, p. 9.

12 Carl F. Kaestle, *Pillars of the Republic: Common Schools and American Society, 1780-1860* (New York: Hill and Wang, 1983), p. 126.

13 Quoted in Geraldine Joncich Clifford, "Man/Woman/Teacher: Gender, Family and Career in American Educational History," *American Teachers: Histories of a Profession at Work*, ed. Donald Warren (New York: Macmillan Publishing Co., 1989), p. 300.

14 Kaestle, p. 125.

15 Quoted in Clifford, p. 305.

16 Dee Ann Spencer, "The Personal Lives of Women Teachers: An Intergenerational View," *Teacher Education Quarterly*, 14 (Spring, 1987) as discussed in Martin, p. 21.

17 See Wayne J. Urban, *Why Teachers Organized* (Detroit: Wayne State University Press, 1982); Wayne J. Urban, "Teacher Activism," *American Teachers: Histories of a Profession at Work*, ed. Donald Warren (New York: Macmillan Publishing Co., 1989).

18 Urban, "Teacher Activism," p. 193.

19 Joel Spring, *American Education: An Introduction to Social and Political Aspects* (New York: Longman, 1989), p. 238.

20 Urban, "Teacher Activism," p. 194.

21 *Ibid.*, p. 195.

22 *Ibid.*, p. 198.

23 Jurgen Herbst, "Teacher Preparation in the Nineteenth Century: Institutions and Purposes," *American Teachers: Histories of a Profession at Work*, ed. Donald Warren (New York: Macmillan Publishing Co., 1989), p. 218.

24 The University of Tennessee, Board of Trustees Minutes, 1891.

25 Herbst, p. 220.

26 Clinton B. Allison, "Training Dixie's Teachers: The University of Tennessee's Summer Normal Institutes," *Journal of Thought*, 18 (Fall, 1983).

27 David Tyack, "The Future of the Past: What Do We Need to Know About the History of Teaching," *American Teachers: Histories of a Profession at Work*, ed. Donald Warren (New York: Macmillan Publishing Co., 1989), p. 412.

28 Mabel W. Hardin, "Teacher-Training in High School," (unpublished Masters thesis, University of Tennessee, 1923).

29 Herbst, p. 226.

30 *Ibid.*

31 *Tennessee School Report*, 1894, p. 206.

32 Herbst, p. 230.

33 Nel Noddings, "Feminist Critiques in the Professions," *Review of Research in Education*, 16 (1990) American Educational Research Associ-

ation Yearbook, pp. 393, 416; David Tyack and Elizabeth Hansot, *Learning Together: A History of Coeducation in American Public Schools* (New York: Russell Sage Foundation, 1992), p. 282.

34 Glorianne M. Leck, "Examining Gender as a Foundation Within Foundational Studies," 91 (Spring, 1990), *Teachers College Record*, pp. 385-387; Noddings, p. 393; Tyack and Hansot, p. 282.

35 Leck, pp. 392, 415; Tyack and Hansot, p. 283.

36 Noddings, p. 400.

37 Joan C. Williams, "Deconstructing Gender," *Feminist Jurisprudence: The Difference Debate*, ed. Leslie Friedman Goldstein (Rowman & Littlefield Publishers, 1992), pp. 46, 48, 71.

38 *Ibid*, p. 47.

39 Jerry Bellon, C. A. Kershaw, E. C. Bellon, and D. J. G. Brian, *A Study of Factors Related to Quality of Worklife in Educational Settings*, Paper presented to Annual Meeting of the American Educational Research Association, (New Orleans, 1988).

IV

The Governance of American Education: Who Controls the Public Schools?

In discussions of the governance of public schools, one of the most common, if thoughtless, sentiments is: *Get the schools out of politics*. Teachers, professors, textbook authors, school superintendents, school custodians, and parents seem to be of one mind on this issue. This prescription simply seems unassailable to most Americans; perhaps you agree with it. For what does politics in education lead to according to its detractors: (a) ignorance—persons without knowledge or understanding of children or curriculum making educational decisions based on tradition, prejudice, or superstition; (b) gross favoritism—teachers and principals being hired because of their political connections rather than their qualifications and credentials; (c) corruption—buildings, books, and supplies purchased in exchange for political support; (d) unfairness—the powerful controlling the schools in their interest without regard to the needs of the powerless; and (e) inefficiency—perhaps worst of all—with school administration in the hands of those who lack an understanding of modern school management techniques.

One problem with this apolitical position is that politics is often used as a pejorative term. Rather than *Webster's* first definition: "the art or science of government," when politics is mentioned, many automatically think of something like the third definition: "political activities characterized by artful and often dishonest practices."[1] In this chapter we will use the first meaning of politics as we concern ourselves with who controls the schools and how scarce resources are allocated. If politics is

defined in this way, those who believe in democracy, freedom, and self-rule must have a difficult time disdaining "politics." As we shall see in the historical sections of this chapter, attempts to get schools out of politics have not enhanced democratic decision making but have resulted in increased control by elites. Teachers, particularly, have an obligation to be critical of rather than indifferent to the politics of education and the processes of school governance. Before we get to a historical sketch on the politics of public schools, I will review some contemporary issues related to control of public schools at the local and state levels. (I will discuss the role of the national [federal] government towards the end of the chapter.) The theme of this chapter is the persistence of control of public schools by elites.

In our federal system, control over public schools is shared by local, state, and national governments. Although public schools are usually thought of as a state responsibility under the "reserve clause" of the 10th Amendment to the Constitution, traditionally most of the control of local schools has taken place at the local level. States vary in the structures of their local school systems, but usually policy is established by a board of education consisting of lay persons (rather than professional educators) elected by the voters. And a superintendent of schools, a "professional educator" with graduate degrees in school administration, is either hired by the board or occasionally elected by the voters to administer the schools. The line between policy making and administration is, of course, ambiguous, leading to misunderstandings, bickering, and, on rare but entertaining occasions, brawls between the superintendent and the board.

Local control is not necessarily democratic. Members of boards of education are part of an elite class of society: those having power, privilege, and prestige. Sociological studies going back to the 1920s indicate that they have long consisted of privileged persons.[2] Board members are white, male, middle-aged (if they were gorillas, they would be silverbacks), upper middle-class, college-educated professionals (doctors, lawyers, etc.), business owners, or executives. In a significant change over the past few years, more are women, now about 40 percent, but minority representation (African-American and Latino) has decreased.[3]

Local boards of education represent the formal governance of schools, but much of the influence and power over educational policy in American communities is exerted by power elites who are not necessarily part of the formal governance structure of public schools. The composition of these local elites varies according to the community, but it is usually based on wealth: industrialists or owners and managers of the dominant economic interests, bankers, owners of media, clergy of the churches attended by the affluent. In some communities there may be competition or conflict among power structures, but the political, social, and educational views of these elites tend to be reactionary or conservative rather than liberal; they are almost never radical.[4] Members of these elites who do not serve on school boards belong to the same golf and city clubs as those who do. If they are women, they are likely to belong to the Junior League; if they are men, their wives or daughters do (they went to the same selective colleges and have the same silver patterns). They go to the same parties and other social functions. They have disproportionate influence over school affairs because they have economic power, because they share a value system with members of the board (and often the superintendent), and because they have continuing, informal access to members of the board. Poor and minority citizens lack any of these means of influence.

School superintendents may have working-class or (more often in the past) small family farm origins, but they usually prefer working with elites. Superintendents are often the first generation of their family to be college educated. Their public school teaching experience often included coaching varsity sports (evidence to many in the community that if one is a leader of boys in athletics, he has a potential to be a leader of men and women in education). The future superintendent often earned a masters degree in educational administration while teaching and perhaps a doctor of education degree while serving as a high school principal.

Success in moving from principal of a school to superintendent of schools depends in part on adopting the manners, styles, and perspectives of the local power elite, trading the Sears polyester sport coats for Brooks Brothers wool-blend suits (perhaps helping to explain their frequent preoccupation with dress codes) and improving table manners by paying close attention at Rotary luncheons. Their political views were normally already sufficiently conservative. Some of the rest of their lifestyle changes, especially at the beginning, may have been "just playing the game," but acceptance by the powerful is heady stuff and socialization to the norms of the elite was often eagerly sought. As superintendents, they are often more comfortable with elite rather than poorer board members. Not only do they share value systems about educational issues and policies, but higher status board members are more likely to respect the professional expertise of superintendents (as they respect technical knowledge by experts in their business). Thus, elite board members are less likely than lower socioeconomic class board members to get involved in administrative details, particularly as they relate to specific schools and classrooms.

State control over public schools varies from state to state, but usually includes compulsory attendance requirements, number of days in the school year, minimum curriculum requirements, graduation requirements, teacher certification requirements, and minimum school financial requirements (including the distribution of state and often federal funds). Some states, much to the annoyance of local school officials, have quite detailed requirements about every aspect of local school practices—"they tell us how many urinals to put in the boys' bathrooms."

Although states have been increasing their control over local schools since the common school movement of the mid-nineteenth century, the 1980s was a time of particularly intense political activity by state governments when governors discovered that educational reform was a hot educational issue. A bevy of education reform governors included Democrat Bill Clinton of Arkansas, who parlayed his status as a leader of the nation's school reform governors into his party's presidential nomination with the endorsement of the nation's largest teacher's organization, the National Education Association. Clinton appointed Richard Riley, the education reform governor of South Carolina, U. S. Secretary of Education. Another reform governor, Republican Lamar Alexander of Tennessee (advocate of career ladders and vouchers to private schools) was appointed Secretary of Education by President Bush, much to the dismay of the NEA.

The reform governors emphasized the economic benefits to their state by having quality schools. They espoused human capital theory: better educated citizens produce more wealth and help the United States compete in world markets. The "reforms" included changed certification requirements and merit pay for teachers (often called ladders), reliance on standardized testing of students, and advocacy of school choice or vouchers. These "reforms" or proposals were often opposed by teachers' organizations but supported by business groups. In the often bitter political conflicts between teachers' organizations and business groups, it is not surprising that the governors usually sided with business.

Historical Perspectives

Politics and governance of schools must be considered within the context of the major purposes of education. When the paramount purpose of schools is to produce human capital in order to foster America's place in a world economy, it is not surprising that business interests are the most powerful political force in determining educational policy. On the other hand in the seventeenth century when preparing people to live in a biblical commonwealth and maintaining church discipline were the major goals, clerical control of the schools established by the Old Deluder Satan Act was to be expected.

A postmodern analysis of the politics of schooling should not take the existence of the present system of public schools for granted. They may seem functional to most Americans today; however that does not make them inevitable. Rather, contemporary school systems are the result of historical forces, and there were competing models of schools (in purpose and governance) in existence in early American history. In order to provide historical perspectives, I will review the work of five prominent historians of education who have analyzed different aspects of the politics of American public schooling: Michael B. Katz, David B. Tyack and Elisabeth Hansot, Raymond E. Callahan, and William J. Reese. From time to time, my voice and those of other historians and writers will be heard as well.

Michael B. Katz and Promoters of Bureaucracy

Historian Michael B. Katz has analyzed four competing models of school organization in the new republic. For purposes of analysis, he gave them fancy names: (a) democratic localism, (b) paternalistic voluntarism, (c) corporate voluntarism, and (d) incipient bureaucracy. These models were not only alternative visions of the forms that schooling might take in the United States, they were already existing types of school organization.[5]

Democratic Localism. What Katz calls democratic localism was the most pervasive school organization in the revolutionary and early national periods. Americans of the time knew it as the district school–there were tens of thousands of them. In the North and West, there was one in virtually every white community once the native people had been chased away, or massacred. In New England, district schools were descendants of the town schools that had been established by the Old Deluder Satan Act or similar legislation in other colonies. As the population dispersed and secularism increased (the worst fears of the Puritans of previous generations having been realized), the district schools became the dominant pattern, crossing the Alleghenies and eventually infiltrating the South. An institution which generations of Americans have enshrined through nostalgia, it was the little red school house that made America great. This one-room school was where every boy carved his initials in his desk, every girl got her pigtail dipped in the inkwell (and annoying questions of sexism were unheard of), all the children learned their ABC's to the tune of a hickory stick, and starting a school day without prayer and Bible reading was inconceivable.

If many conservative Americans of past generations suffered fits of nostalgia as they longed after the little red school house, radical scholars have experienced similar symptoms, finding in the district schools the kind of participatory democracy lacking in modern bureaucratic structures. In their ideal district school, members of the local community controlled each school, reflected local values, and responded to local needs. If a community consisted primarily of Baptists, Lutherans, or Catholics, it was only fair and reasonable that the curriculum and the teachers supported that faith. For scholars and educators who despair of schools governed by elites and bureaucrats, district schools can serve as a historical example of the democratic faith that people know what is best for themselves and can manage their own affairs.

But, as Katz points out, democratic localism as exemplified by the district school is a "nostalgic memory" or, at best, a "noble alternative vision" rather than an actual working model of participatory educational democracy: "It embraced a broad and humanistic conception of education as uncharacteristic of nineteenth-century as of twentieth-century schools and schoolmen [or, perhaps, schoolwomen]."[6] First, in practice, it was often the antithesis of democracy with rule by a "tyrannical local majority whose ambition was control and dominance of its own narrow sectarian or political bias in the schoolroom."[7] (Why is it that so many otherwise intelligent and knowledgeable Americans do not understand that democracy and majority rule are not the same thing and that, in many circumstances, they are incompatible?) Katz uses the example of control by the Berkshire Congregational Church of local New England schools, but you can think of many contemporary examples of racial, ethnic, religious, or other majorities who would (or do) engage in tyrannical treatment of minorities if unrestrained by conceptions of minority rights or by courts.

But local control is not synonymous with democracy in other ways. Local minorities in the form of the wealthy (or at least the wealthier) and other elites often exercise community control including control over schools. In the twentieth century, coal operators sometimes dictated school policy in Appalachia; white landowners determined educational opportunities or, more likely, the lack of them for African-Americans in the South; and Anglo minorities decided Spanish was not to be spoken in classrooms where Latinos were a majority in the Southwest. Indeed, those who cry the loudest for local control of public institutions are usually the local elites who oppose "outside interference" with the ways they exercise their power. At the same time, local elites are often able (through a process of hegemony) to convince those who have not been exercising power that local control is democratic.

In the ostensibly democratic district schools of the early republic, local patriarchs were often in charge, selecting the textbooks, buying what meager supplies were absolutely essential, and hiring the teacher. As I pointed out in chapter three, the father figures who controlled these schools were strongly antiprofessional. They expected the young women whom they hired as teachers to do as they were told. They viewed teacher-training institutions, especially normal schools, with hostility. Trained teachers might well be uppity teachers, resistant to control.

Paternalistic Voluntarism. Paternalistic voluntarism was the label given by Michael Katz to another alternative proposal for the organization and governance of "public" schools. As was the case of democratic localism, examples of this type of school organization actually existed, particularly in early nineteenth-century urban areas. These were schools for the poor, controlled and administered by philanthropic groups with names that indicated their class bias: the Philadelphia Society for the Free Instruction of Indigent Boys or the Benevolent Society of the City of Baltimore for the Education of the Female Poor. They were very popular in the Northeast but were also established in what were then western cities, including Cincinnati, Detroit, Dayton, and St. Louis.

The schools reflected voluntarism in that they were administered by private citizens (although they often, as in New York City, used public funds). Katz used the New York Public School Society as a case study, characterizing the Society as "an unpaid, self-perpetuating board of first citizens."[8] The leadership was paternalistic, imbued by a sense of *noblesse oblige*. The children of the poor were educated by their social and economic "betters," and as Katz points out, poor children were not provided with the kind of education that the upper-class members of the Society provided for their own children. Rather, within the context of their own self-interest, the wealthy provided the kind of education that they thought the poor should have. "Make no mistake about it," Katz writes, "this was a class system of education. It provided a vehicle for the efforts of one class to civilize another and thereby ensure that society would remain tolerable, orderly, and safe."[9]

The schools that were established by the philanthropic societies were usually monitorial schools, often called Lancastrian schools for Joseph Lancaster who claimed to have invented them. Their purpose was to give instruction in elementary reading, writing, arithmetic, and morality (particularly docility and obedience) to the children of the poor. The parents often had to take a pauper oath before their children were admitted, swearing that they did not have the money to pay tuition to school their children. Teaching behavior and attitudes thought to be appropriate for the working class was part of the hidden curriculum and was facilitated by the organization of the schools. In some cases, several hundred students were taught by one schoolmaster who used older students as monitors. Lancaster prepared a detailed guide for monitorial schools. Such detail was necessary because the system could work only if a rigid curriculum was followed using teaching methods of military precision—a structure much like a factory, thus an appropriate education for future factory workers.[10]

The education was clearly inferior to that provided to more affluent children. The student-teacher ratio of one to several hundred was undesirable by any standard, particularly at a time when the prevailing teaching method was oral recitation. An English visitor to a monitorial school in St. Louis said the noise of the students reciting aloud reminded him of a riot in a parrot house. However, the monitorial system was very inexpensive, a major consideration in the education of the poor, then and now. Lancaster not only promoted the cheapness of his plan because of the savings of hiring only one master, he suggested savings in the use of supplies. As an example, writing slates could be dispensed with; students and their monitor could gather around sand piles, writing their letters and numbers with a stick in the sand.

With hundreds of students in one space, discipline was obviously a problem. The discipline proposals of Lancaster were severe with specific penalties suggested for different infractions. He based his techniques on the use of humiliation and shame. As an example, he suggested that an incorrigible student be placed in a basket that would be pulled up to the rafters of the schoolhouse and tied above the rest of the students (monitorial schools were necessarily open, barn-like structures).

When people are abused by institutions they usually find ways to resist. Students and parents resisted in about the only way open to them; they voted against the school societies with their feet. Many children stopped going to school. Bishop Hughes of New York claimed that the schools administered by the Public School Society were anti-Catholic and anti-poor, alienating parents so much that many refused to send their children. The members of the society responded, according to Hughes, by requesting "a legal enactment . . . to compel an attendance" These legal enactments would deprive parents of public relief (welfare) if they didn't send their children to school, and requested that employers not hire persons who refused to send their children to school.[11]

Corporate Voluntarism. Katz calls a third model corporate voluntarism. It was to be found in academies and colleges, controlled by boards of trustees and financed through endowments, tuitions, and sometimes, by public funds—especially income derived from public lands. From the late eighteenth to the late nineteenth centuries, academies were the dominant type of secondary school in the United States. Academies replaced or supplemented the Latin Grammar Schools which had been mandated in New England towns by colonial acts such as the Old Deluder Satan Act. By the beginning of the twentieth century, the academies were losing their dominant position in secondary education to public high schools.

According to Katz, corporate voluntarism in the form of academies was supported in the early republic, in part, because it provided a good deal of educational freedom. These schools were "public" in the sense that the term was used at the time:

> performance of broad social functions and the service of a large, heterogeneous, nonexclusive clientele rather than control and ownership by the community or state. . . . Although managed and owned by self-

> perpetuating boards of trustees, academies were profoundly public institutions.[12]

Such schools experienced little government interference, and academies of many different types "suited to varying tastes" were established, a system of "mild anarchy" in contrast to the standardization that was to come later.[13]

Incipient Bureaucracy. According to Katz, the fourth of the alternative organizational models, incipient bureaucracy, triumphed.[14] By incipient bureaucracy, he means the establishment of state-wide *systems* of public schools, the prevailing type of schooling in America today and an institution celebrated by educational historians until attacks in the 1960s and 1970s when school systems were accused of being bureaucratic, racist, and class biased. According to this leftist critique, the schools were unresponsive to the poor, systematically denying them an adequate education. In the 1980s and 1990s, the far right also attacked the public school bureaucracies, charging them with being unresponsive to the public at large and generally failing to provide an adequate education for Americans.

Katz finds incipient bureaucracy in the common school systems created in mid-nineteenth century. The common school was a product of the city because the district school did not work well in an urban environment. Multiple separate school districts in one city were inefficient and squandered scarce resources on the duplication of facilities. The inequities among rich and poor districts were too pronounced to be politically acceptable. (Although even a cursory examination of public schools in rich and poor parts of almost any American city will show that inequities remain, in Jonathan Kozol's phrase, "savage.")[15]

Common school systems were also a consequence of ideology. Katz and other revisionist historians argue that the common school leaders who created state-wide systems of public schools wanted standardization and systematization of schools because they wanted to make sure that modern, industrial values were taught to the children of the working class, a point discussed more fully in chapter five on poverty and education.

Katz calls the common school leaders "promoters of bureaucracy."[16]

David B. Tyack, Elisabeth Hansot, and the Promoters of Virtue

As indicated in my discussion of the aims of education in chapter one, the common school leaders were primarily interested in the inculcation of proper values in the young. Perhaps better than promoters of bureaucracy, they should be called promoters of virtue. Tyack and Hansot entitle their book on public school leadership in America, *Managers of Virtue*.[17] Using National Education Association obituaries, they analyze the common school promoters:

> the school leader was an expert mainly in the formation of moral character. . . . Coming largely from respectable but hardly affluent middle-class families—like the twentieth-century school superintendents who succeeded them—they saw themselves as upholders of stern standards of individual morality and a common denominator of civic virtue in a mobile, rapidly changing economic and social order.[18]

Studies of school board members in the West at the time show similar patterns. They were more socially prominent and more prosperous than ordinary settlers.[19] Thus, the generalization made in the introduction of this chapter: from the time of their creation, local public schools have been governed by elites, rather than by a cross-section of ordinary citizens. The Protestant-republican-capitalist views of school leaders were to be inculcated into every person's child. Rather than a private affair, the teaching of values through public schools was a function of government. The "father" of the public schools, Horace Mann, exemplified this attitude. "Like many other Whig politicians," Tyack and Hansot write, Mann "believed it a virtue to mind other people's business."[20]

One of the most interesting (and disturbing) characteristics of nineteenth-century school leaders was to see other values as simply wrong: they didn't get the idea of pluralism. They took their own values as self-evident—as the real American values. Other ideologies were perversions, and the public schools, obviously, should teach the truth. They had little basis for understanding the desertion of Catholics, who were bitter about Yankee-Protestant indoctrination, from the public school system.

The centralized, hierarchical, bureaucratic school structures that we know (and only educational bureaucrats seem to admire) emerged at the turn of the twentieth century. These bureaucratic school systems reflected the changes that were taking place in other institutions in that era, particularly the growth of gigantic business enterprises and, after sometimes idiosyncratic control by their founders, the adoption of corporate models of administration. This was, after all, the age of the captains of industry (as they were called by those who admired the businessmen who were the most powerful force in American life) or the robber barons (the name given by those who disliked them). Perhaps even more so than today (although with the recent Perot phenomenon, this is hard saying), the multimillionaires such as the Rockefellers, Carnegies, and Vanderbilts symbolized successful leaders in modern America.[21]

As is true of social movements generally, the standardization and centralization of schools can be understood in several ways. Traditionally, educational historians have applauded. They have found virtue in consolidation of schools, small and nonpartisan school boards, age grading, uniform standards for schools, and (at the same time) differentiated curricula (vocational education and programs for the disabled, among others), training of educational experts, and corporate forms of administration. Traditional historians have included these changes in the broader progressive movement in education. According to its proponents, a major improvement was taking school administration "out of politics"; decisions would be made by educational experts, trained in the new educational science rather than by self-seeking politicians with one eye on voting blocs and the other on easy money. Consistent and equitable treatment of students resulted from administrative reforms, according to this interpretation. "Theoretically at least," Tyack writes, "issues of religion or ethnicity were irrelevant to decision making in such bureaucracies, as were parochial tastes or local prejudices."[22] Graft would be eliminated as big-city school administrators, too often appointed by political bosses, would be replaced by professionally trained experts in educational management. Perhaps most importantly, schools would become more efficient. In modernity, there is no greater virtue than efficiency.

We certainly should not look on the administrative reforms of the early twentieth century as neutral. Tyack warns: "It was very important not to portray this kind of organizational change as an inevitable process. Some people helped to plan the changes and benefited from them, others did not; some results were intended, others were not. Schools are rarely so politically neutral as they portray themselves."[23] As in all change, there were winners and losers. And, according to revisionist historians, the winners here, as in progressive reforms generally, were the cosmopolitan elite (in large part an affluent urban, upper-middle class). In Robert Wiebe's words it was "the ambition of the new middle class to fulfill its destiny through bureaucratic means."[24] Revisionist historians have been particularly critical of the progressive reforms of urban school boards. The old, large, ward-based school boards (that Katz characterized as democratic localism) were replaced with small (seven members being common), nonpartisan school boards elected at large from throughout a city. The result was, of course, that only an elite could wage successful campaigns for election. Increasingly, school boards consisted of those who were called the "better class of men." Tyack analyzes the consequences:

> When administrative progressives succeeded in doing this by changing city charters . . . they often blocked the political channels by which the cities' working-class and ethnic communities had traditionally expressed their political interests in education. In the process they also enhanced the power of cosmopolitan elites.[25]

As indicated before, small, elite school boards, used to the corporate model of decision making, are more likely to rely on professional experts for making day-to-day and technical decisions, increasing the power of superintendents who claimed that their graduate work in educational science made them such experts. Thus, the move to small, nonpartisan school boards did not get the schools out of politics. It further shifted the political power to economic elites and to school administrators.

Early twentieth-century school administrators pictured themselves as educational scientists, experts in bringing social efficiency to schooling, but they were also moralists. Much like the religious right today, they contrasted the virtues of an idealized rural past with the value conflicts in a resented pluralistic present. And like their counterparts today, they were eager to use the schools to shape the values of the unguided and the misguided. Particularly in need from their point of view were the millions of immigrant children to be Americanized. In the name of social efficiency and moral superiority, the new professional school administrators guarded their decision-making power from both the public and teachers at the local level.

Raymond E. Callahan and the Cult of Efficiency

Raymond Callahan wrote a classic book on the attempts of school administrators to use the methods of "scientific management," much in vogue in business in the early twentieth century.[26] Callahan summed up the consequences of the application of business "values and practices" in schools: "Regardless of the motivation, the consequences for American education and American society were tragic."[27] Two interrelated factors were largely responsible for the acceptance of business management methods in educational administration: the vulnerability of school superintendents to the loss of their jobs and the enchantment with business and wealth in early twentieth-century America. Because superintendents (then and now) are subject to conflicting community values and are held responsible for social problems over which they have little control, they have distressingly short tenure, frequently less than three or four years in urban school systems. Even more than now, the early twentieth-century school superintendent worked in a culture that exalted business and businessmen (in the age of the suffragettes, the gender bias within the dominant business culture was barely challenged). President Calvin Coolidge captured the spirit of the era with his famous dictum that the "business of America is business." It is not surprising that vulnerable school superintendents adopted "business-industrial management" values and techniques. Given their conservative rural backgrounds, their lack of an intellectual, scholarly study of education, and the fact that they were at the mercy of school board members (whom, as I have belabored, promoted the industrial ethic), it would have been surprising had they done otherwise. One of the unfortunate aspects of their historical development is that school administrators often have a strong streak of anti-intellectualism. They tend to be impatient with theoretical and philosophical discussions of educational policy. In the male-oriented language of a previous era, "They regarded the scholar as a harmless but inept fellow, their models were not the thinkers such as the Deweys, the Beards, or the Veblens but the men of action–the Fords and the Carnegies."[28]

Enthusiastic professors of school administration borrowed the principles of scientific management to create a pseudo-science of education decision-making. Using the terminology of business, they talked of "per pupil cost," "school plant," "respective products," and "investment per pupil."[29] One of the most influential of these professors, Frank Spaulding of Yale University, argued that even the monetary value of subjects in the curriculum could be determined scientifically. Developing an elaborate formula (based primarily on costs), he determined in one secondary school "that 5.9 pupil-recitations in Greek are of the same value as 23.8 pupil-recitations in French; that 12 pupil-recitations in science are equivalent in value to 19.2 pupil-recitations in English; and that it takes 41.7 pupil-recitations in vocal music to equal the value of 13.9 pupil-recitations in art."[30]

At the very beginning of their profession, the role that superintendents chose was that of school executive rather than instruction and curriculum specialist or educational philosopher. Callahan argues that the tragic consequences were fourfold:

> Educational questions were subordinated to business considerations . . . administrators were produced who were not, in any true sense, educators . . . a scientific label was put on some very unscientific and dubious methods and practices; and . . . an anti-intellectual climate, already prevalent, was strengthened.[31]

One of the peculiarities of our society is that despite the numerous and highly publicized moral and ethical lapses of business executives as well as the frequent failures of their products to compete in a global economy, many Americans continue to call for a larger role for business methods and "businessmen" in public schools. The "effective schools research" indicates that principals of effective schools spend more time on matters of curriculum and instruction and less on fiscal and physical plant issues.[32] Yet, one of my legislators in Tennessee recently introduced a bill that would have required principals to have a Masters of Business Administration degree.

William J. Reese and Grass-roots Reform

Anything of consequence can be understood in more than one way. Traditional educational historians saw the administrative progressives as promoting professionalism and efficiency. Revisionist historians saw them promoting bureaucracy and indoctrinating youth with the values an elite wished them to have. Recently, critical historians have developed more complicated interpretations. Critical theorists, including critical historians, emphasize human agency: people are not just victims of forces and movements created by elites. People have the power to resist–to reject or modify that which is being imposed by the powerful. An excellent example of this type of interpretation is William J. Reese's, *Power and the Promise of School Reform: Grass-roots Movements During the Progressive Era.*[33]

Reese pictures the progressive reforms as a series of conflicts ("efficiency versus democracy, freedom versus control") among a variety of interest groups consisting of business elites but also grassroots reformers (labor unions, liberal women's groups, socialists, social gospellers, and Populists). In many cases, they supported the same reforms (the school health movement or vacation schools as examples) but usually for very different reasons. For the most part, however, these grassroots reformers opposed the centralization of ward school boards into small, "non-partisan" boards.

Reese points out that urban school boards, even before centralization (and the installing of "professional" administrators), were controlled by elite classes. Before 1890, in three of the cities he used as case studies (Rochester, Toledo, and Milwaukee), no unskilled laborers, women, or African-Americans served on school boards.[34] School boards before and after the progressive reforms were made up of white male businessmen and professionals.

According to Reese, grassroots reformers were not deceived by the administrative progressives who promised nonpartisan school governance; they saw it as "an ideological cloak" by the elite:[35]

> The triumph of business reform in the schools was never complete during the Progressive era, largely because of the activist stance of Socialists, Progressive workers, liberal women, and other groups that had surfaced during the depression of the 1890s.[36]

Bureaucratic control of public schools by centralized, "nonpartisan" boards and "professional" administrators was resisted, sometimes vigorously. Bureaucratic organization spread unevenly, coming much more slowly to isolated, rural areas. Nevertheless, by the middle of the twentieth century, it was the prevailing form of school organization in the United States.

The Federal Government and the Politics of Education

Thus far I have concentrated on politics and governance of schools at the local and state levels where most of the control lies. Since World War II, however, the influence and power of the national government have increased and we need to direct some attention to it. Following World War II, there was a debate (sometimes bitter) about the constitutionality of a larger role for the national government in public schools, particularly in financial support. Public schools were neglected even more than usual during the depression years of the "dirty thirties" and the war years of the forties.[37] School buildings were often incredibly primitive (outdoor privies were still common in rural areas), resembling the world of the nineteenth century more than the twentieth. Rural or urban buildings were inadequate and frequently worn out. Younger teachers had been siphoned off by the military or better-paying jobs in the defense industry. However dedicated, those who were left were often old and inadequately educated, frequently nondegreed graduates of normal schools.

The tasks faced by the schools were formidable. There was the sheer number of students to educate. In the years following the war, the baby boom created the most distinctive demographic feature of the second half of the twentieth century. The public schools were simply inadequate to meet the requirements for technically educated persons in the new era. A changing, industrial economy had a vociferous appetite for scientists, engineers, and technological workers. The cold war would soon bring forth cries of anguish that Ivan knew physics and Johnnie didn't (no one seemed to care about Janice); as a consequence, we were going to lose the weapons race with the Soviet Union.

In the late 1940s, inflation was rampant, social needs caused by the dislocations of war were pressing, and many local governments lacked the resources to reconstruct their school systems. According to their critics, public school bureaucrats generally lacked the will to exchange the progressive pap in the public for tough, scholarly study of the disciplines. One response was to look to the power and financial resources of the national government, raising constitutional questions as well as issues of federal control—both particularly frightening specters for conservatives.

The conventional argument by the opponents of federal aid to education was that it was simply unconstitutional. Education is not mentioned in the Constitution, so the founding fathers must not have wanted the national government to get involved. The opponents of federal aid argued that education was one of those activities retained by the states under the reserve clause of the tenth amendment. To be sure, some national aid had always been provided through land grants to support education generally, or federal funds for agricultural or industrial education. But this aid was never enough to directly challenge the implicit constitutional prohibition. Actually, the small role that the national government played in public schooling until after W. W. II was not so much because federal aid was against the American Constitution as it was against the American culture. At the time the Constitution was written, Americans lived in a pre-schooling society. Most were educated by institutions other than schools. Even where schools existed, they were in church or private hands; nowhere in the English-speaking world was schooling a function of government. It would have been anachronistic for the Constitution to have addressed a national role for schooling. Such was not the case by the mid-twentieth century.

In the twentieth century, advocates of federal aid to education had generally been liberals. Conservatives viewed the very idea of federal aid with alarm. The National Association of Manufacturers, the National Chamber of Commerce, and the Roman Catholic Church were among the most vociferous opponents. (The opposition of the Catholics led to a continuing, nasty debate between the quintessential liberal, Eleanor Roosevelt, and Cardinal Spellman, Archbishop of New York.)[38] Catholics were implacable in their opposition to federal aid if it went only to public schools, and in that era, it was unthinkable that public funds could be spent on parochial schools.

Federal aid to education was enacted only when a broad consensus that included elite business interests was formed. A number of elements led to the consensus: (a) the almost universal approval of the Servicemen's Readjustment Act of 1944 (the GI Bill that allowed millions of veterans to attend college) as an example of the positive benefits of such aid, (b) a many-sided attack on the anti-intellectualism of public schools which could be rectified only by circumventing professional educators, (c) and the launching of the first satellite in space (Sputnik I) by the Soviet Union in 1957. Sputnik may have been most important because it could be used as a symbol of the failure of our public schools to produce the mathematicians and scientists need to win the space race and, perhaps, even the cold war.

Much of the debate about the public schools in the 1950s sounds familiar to those who have been listening to current criticisms of education–in both cases, schools were to be a major force in winning wars against threats to the American way of life. In the cold war of the 1950s, the enemy was godless communism as exemplified by the Soviet Union and its military power. In the global economy of the 1980s and 1990s, the enemy was the economic power of Japan and Western Europe and their effective use of human capital. In both cases, critics denounced public schools for their academic shortcomings, particularly their failure to teach mathematics and science adequately. In the cold war period, the demand was for scientists and engineers who could help compete successfully with the

Soviet Union in technology, especially in weapons systems. At any rate, sufficient conservatives were won over by the national defense argument and the National Defense Education Act was passed in 1958, providing the first large-scale federal funds for public schooling. Funds from the bill supported science, mathematics, and modern foreign languages. President Lyndon Johnson was also able to pass the Elementary and Secondary Education Act in 1965, providing funds to aid his "War on Poverty." Since then the federal contributions to local school budgets has averaged about seven percent. But wide-spread allegiance to the slogan of "local control" has kept the federal government from much direct involvement in the governance of local schools. The role of the federal government has been primarily hortatory: pleading, challenging, and sometimes threatening local schools into following whatever policies the current president and his secretary of education think will save the nation.

Conclusion

Teachers who wish to do good work cannot ignore the politics of education. Political decisions are the way scarce resources are allocated and ideas translated into policies. In a democratic, pluralistic society, political debates are rarely resolved. They reappear generation after generation in altered form and language.

The theme of this chapter has been the persistence of control by elites in school governance. What Katz called democratic localism still retains its appeal, and there are a number of experiments in restructuring schools to make their governance more democratic. Site-based management, charter schools, and choice are the most wide-spread of these experiments. Site-based management is being tried across the country, but the school councils of Chicago have received the most attention. In Chicago, councils in individual schools consist of ten persons: six parents, two teachers, and two community representatives. The council has "the power to hire and dismiss principals, approve budgets, and make recommendations on the curriculum and textbooks. . . . For the first time in the twentieth century," historian Joel Spring writes, "a political means was available to the average Chicago citizen for influencing local schools."[39] Unlike in Chicago, teachers and school administrators have most of the power in a number of site-based management plans. There are also now hundreds of charter schools designed by parents and teachers in the United States. Charter schools are publicly funded but operate under contracts with boards of education rather than under their direct control.

Variations on the forms that Michael B. Katz called paternalistic voluntarism and corporate voluntarism are part of the debate over vouchers (proponents prefer "choice," as more politically attractive) where tax funds are used to support an alternative to public schools. Paternalistic voluntarism as a historical precedent in education might provoke us to reflect on issues of private versus public responsibility and control of basic human services. Conservatives often support policies of privatization of traditional public responsibilities and of a shift from government responsibility for health, education, and welfare programs to a greater role for private charities. The New York Public School Society may be viewed as a nineteenth-century example of one of former President Bush's "thousand points of light." It had many of the same problems as the privately-controlled human service agencies do today: it had a pauper or charity stigma attached to it, it provided a vastly unequal education, and it lacked accountability to the people who used it. Public responsibility for delivering basic human services has not been a panacea—social class biases remain pervasive and bureaucrats are too often maddening—but relying on private control often exacerbates these problems. Nevertheless, in a number of American cities, private companies have contracted with public officials to administer schools. One of former Secretary of Education Lamar Alexander's friends and political allies, Chris Whittle of Whittle Communications (creator of Channel One that brings a news program and commercials into public school classrooms) created the Edison Project, a private corporation to administer schools with public funds.

We may be witnessing a resurgence of corporate voluntarism in American education today. Over the past twenty-five years, more and more students have been enrolled in academies and day schools, often operated by churches and other religious organizations. In the 1960s and 1970s, civil rights groups and public school advocates often argued that these academies were established to avoid racial integration—indeed, they were sometimes called segregationist academies by their detractors. Undoubtedly, some were established for this reason. However, it has become increasingly clear that many conservative parents have chosen private rather than public schools because they object to the values they perceive as characterizing public schools, both in the behavior of students and in the content of the curriculum which they charge is based on a philosophy (or even a religion) of secular humanism.[40]

In addition, some critics simply charge that the public schools fail to educate. Students don't learn the basic skills or the fundamental content of the disciplines—they leave public schools functionally and culturally illiterate—and this sad state of affairs is the fault of the public school bureaucracy, including teachers. Many of these critics argue that parents and students should have a choice to remain in the failed public schools or to attend private or parochial schools with tax dollars paying all or part of the tuition. The supporters of these voucher systems argue that competition with private schools will help "shape up" public schools. Among the powerful advocates of voucher systems are former President Bush and former Secretary of Education Alexander. In response to his critics who charge that a voucher system would destroy public education, Alexander has argued that perhaps we need to redefine the meaning of a public institution as one that serves public purposes and is accountable to the public. Actually, this meaning of public is quite like the meaning of the term in the eighteenth and nineteenth centuries when academies flourished.

What Katz called incipient bureaucracy grew into full-fledged bureaucracies, a development aided by cries to get schools out of politics. Upper-middle-class, business-oriented school board members take their world view so for granted they often fail to recognize that they are attempting to impose a particular ideology on school children. As an example, the paramount goal of the school to produce efficient workers is accepted matter-of-factly by persons of their social class and business orientation.

They are often blind to the social-class bias and racism involved in differentiated curricula for workers and managers (vocational education versus college preparatory, as an example) or in academic tracking. They have a difficult time understanding resistance by the poor or by African-Americans and other minority groups and often see dissident groups as ignorant or as victims of nefarious political agitators. I discuss these issues of class and race more fully in chapters five and six.

Notes

1 *Webster's Ninth New Collegiate Dictionary* (Springfield, MA: Merriam-Webster, Inc., 1990).

2 George S. Counts, *The Social Composition of Boards of Education: A Study in the Social Control of Public Education* (Chicago: University of Chicago Press, 1927).

3 Beatrice H. Cameron, Kenneth E. Underwood, and Jim C. Fortune, "It's Ten Years Later and You've Hardly Changed at All," *American School Board Journal, 175* (January 1988), p. 20, as summarized in Joseph W. Newman, *America's Teachers: An Introduction to Education* (New York: Longman, 1990), p. 221.

4 See Donald McCarty and Charles Ramsey, *The School Managers: Power and Conflict in American Public Education* (Westport, CT: Greenwood Press, 1971).

5 Michael B. Katz, *Alternative Proposals for American Education: The Nineteenth Century* (New York: Praeger Publishers, 1971).

6 *Ibid.*, pp. 20 and 21.

7 *Ibid.*, p. 20.

8 *Ibid.*, p. 8.

9 *Ibid.*, p. 9.

10 For an interesting account and documents from the period, see Carl F. Kaestle (ed.), *Joseph Lancaster and the Monitorial School Movement: A Documentary History*, Classics in Education, No. 47 (New York: Teachers College Press, 1973).

11 Katz, p. 13.

12 *Ibid.*, p. 23.

13 *Ibid.*, p. 27.

14 *Ibid.*, p. 28.

15 Jonathan Kozol, *Savage Inequalities: Children in America's Schools* (New York: Crown Publishers, 1991); Katz, p. 29.

16 Katz, p. 28.

17 David Tyack and Elisabeth Hansot, *Managers of Virtue: Public School Leadership in America, 1820-1980* (New York: Basic Books, 1982).

18 *Ibid.*, pp. 46, 47.

19 *Ibid.*, p. 53.

20 *Ibid.*, p. 58.

21 For a number of short, interesting essays on the fundamental changes that were taking place in American society in the late nineteenth century, see Ray Ginger, *The Nationalizing of American Life, 1877-1900* (New York, The Free Press, 1965).

22 David B. Tyack, "Ways of Seeing: An Essay on the History of Compulsory Schooling," *Harvard Educational Review*, 46 (August, 1976), p. 374.

23 *Ibid.*, p. 376.

24 Quoted in Tyack, "Ways of Seeing," p. 375.

25 Tyack and Hansot, *Managers of Virtue*, p. 107.

26 Raymond E. Callahan, *Education and the Cult of Efficiency* (Chicago, The University of Chicago Press, 1962); for a current reevaluation of Callahan's interpretation see *Shaping the Superintendency: A Reexamination of Callahan and the Cult of Efficiency*, ed. William Edward Eaton (New York: Teachers College Press, 1990).

27 Callahan, p. 244.

28 *Ibid.*, p. 248.

29 *Ibid.*, p. 71.

30 *Ibid.*, p. 73.

31 *Ibid.*, p. 246.

32 Wilbur B. Brookover, *Effective Secondary Schools* (Philadelphia: Research for Better Schools, 1981).

33 William J. Reese, *Power and the Promise of School Reform: Grass-roots Movements During the Progressive Era* (Boston: Routledge & Kegan Paul, 1986).

34 *Ibid.*, p. 73.

35 *Ibid.*, p. 89.

36 *Ibid.*, p. 115.

37 See David Tyack, Robert Lowe, and Elisabeth Hansot, *Public Schools in Hard Times: The Great Depression and Recent Years* (Cambridge, MA: Harvard University Press, 1984).

38 The story of "The First Lady and the Cardinal" is told in Willis Rudy, *Schools in an Age of Mass Culture: The Exploration of Selected Themes in the History of Twentieth-Century American Education* (Englewood Cliffs, NJ: Prentice-Hall, 1965).

39 Joel Spring, *American Education* (New York: McGraw-Hill, 1994), p. 176.

40 A good account of the Christian day school movement is found in James G. Carper and Thomas C. Hunt (eds.), *Religious Schooling in America,* (Birmingham, AL: Religious Education Press, 1984). A fascinating story of a particular Christian day school is Alan Peshkin's *God's Choice: The Total World of a Fundamentalist Christian School* (Chicago: University of Chicago Press, 1986).

V

Poverty and Education: Do Schools Reproduce Social Class Bias in America?

Discussion of social class is uncomfortable for most Americans; religion, politics, and even sex are more acceptable topics for conversations. "The word class is fraught with unpleasing associations, so that to linger upon it is apt to be interpreted as the symptom of a perverted mind and a jaundiced spirit," Tawney wrote in 1931.[1] Little about class inquiry has changed since. Those who are interested in social class in America are often placed in one of two "undesirable" categories: snobs or Marxists. Nevertheless, America is a society in which social class matters a great deal. As you were taught in Sociology 101, social class involves more than money: classes attach very different meanings to cultural symbols. But in America, income is the most significant determinate of class. The top 20 percent of families receive over 40 percent of the total income of Americans, and the bottom 20 percent receive less than 5 percent; and the disparities are growing. More distressing for those concerned with children, 20 percent of American children are living in poverty. This is the highest rate among industrial nations. Five-and-a-half million children suffer from malnutrition. Call it hunger. According to the U. S. Department of Education, approximately 220,000 school-aged children are among the homeless. Other sources suggest the figure should be closer to 500,000. Many of these children are not even enrolled in school.[2]

American public schools are supposed to meliorate the effects of poverty by, at the very least, providing the young with equal opportunity for an education which will help them climb a ladder of vertical mobility. Too often, schools help reproduce the inequalities in the social order–through funding, the formal curriculum, the "hidden curriculum," and the "lived culture" of students and teachers.

First let's look at funding. Generally in America, rich kids go to plush schools, public or private, schools with omnipresent computers, landscaping, and toilets that work–and are cleaned. These schools remind wealthy children and youth that they are privileged, that they are important. Poor kids usually go to schools that reflect the poverty and hopelessness of their lives. In *Savage Inequalities*, Jonathan Kozol takes us inside schools in poverty neighborhoods and demands that we look at the places children are compelled to go. He takes us to a boys' bathroom in East Saint Louis:

> Four of the six toilets do not work. The toilet stalls, which are eaten away by red and brown corrosion, have no doors. The toilets have no seats. One has a rotten wooden stump. There are no paper towels and no soap. Near the door there is a loop of wire with an empty toilet-paper roll.[3]

Across the country, in Camden, New Jersey, a reading teacher is housed in a coat room, another in a pantry; two teachers hold classes in converted coal bins, and a guidance counselor meets with parents in a closet.[4] These are urban schools, but the same kind of "savage inequalities" may be found in poor rural districts throughout the country. Some of the worst are in Appalachia just a few miles from the university where I teach. In schools which children of poverty attend, the quality (or even availability) of textbooks and other teaching materials is usually as appalling as the physical plants. Much of the difference is a *matter of money*. Even in the same state, much more money is spent per pupil in public schools that rich kids attend. As an example, in 1988-89, the above-mentioned Camden, New Jersey, spent $3,538 per student in school, whereas the public schools of the Princeton school district, a few miles away, spent $7,725. In my home state of Tennessee, prosperous Oak Ridge spends $5,538 per student while Crockett County spends $2,732.[5]

But there is something more than buildings and materials; the very ethos of a school is class determined. In *Horace's Compromise*, Theodore Sizer comments on it:

> Among schools there was one important difference, which followed from a single variable only: the social class of the student body. If the school principally served poor adolescents, its character, if not its structure, varied from sister schools for the more affluent. It got so I could say with some justification to school principals, tell me about the income of your students' families and I'll describe to you your school.[6]

Formal and Hidden Curriculums

The formal and hidden curriculums of schools both reflect and help maintain the social-class position of the students. In the formal curriculum, the school knowledge that is esteemed reflects the culture of the privileged, particularly privileged males, rather than the culture of the working class, minorities, or females. The curriculums in history and literature, for example, are centered on the lives of upper- and upper-middle-class Anglo-European or white American males, adding to the advantage of upper-middle class white children. They are the ones with the useful "cultural capital" (including the use of standard English) to spend in school. Lower-class children, disadvantaged in such a curriculum, can be placed or guided into lower academic tracks or vocational curriculums, limiting their futures  and maintaining their lower status in society. Moreover, the hidden curriculums—the messages contained in the rules, regulations, rituals, and organization of schools—with its emphasis on regularity, punctuality, respect for authority, tolerance for boredom, etc., can be used to teach lower-class children and youth how to behave so that they will better fit into existing social and economic arrangements, including low-paying jobs. On the other hand, the "lived experience" of the students suggests that they often do not behave in ways prescribed by schools, that school is often a contested terrain between students, teachers, and school officials, a point that I will return to in the conclusion of this chapter.[7]

Educational sociologist Lois Weis argues that teachers must be sensitized to their role in encouraging inequality. She emphasizes, quite correctly I think, "that most teachers (and prospective teachers) do not consciously encourage inequalities through schools." In fact, she continues, "many are quite surprised at their own potential and actual role in this process."[8]

With trepidation, I thought back on my own public school teaching. Did I unknowingly foster social class bias? Two embarrassing examples came immediately to mind—I don't want to remember others. First, in my second year of teaching, all sections of American history in my high school were tracked for the first time. Armed with grades in academic classes, standardized test scores, and memories of how well students had "performed" in our classes, the faculty sorted all of the eleventh graders into classes from "advanced placement" to "slow learners." The top tracks were taught by the department head, a wonderful teacher—bright, well-informed, charming, fun. He fostered a questioning attitude about the American past, and his students loved him. The lower tracks were taught by a former school principal who had proved incompetent as an administrator and was serving out his last few years before retirement. He spent most of his class time sitting at his desk staring (or glaring) at the students as they "answered the questions at the back of the chapter." They hated him.

Discussing with six of my colleagues where students should be placed, I felt like a true professional. With one exception, all of these teachers were liberal-minded; several were outspoken advocates of social justice; and a couple of us were active in the local open-housing campaign, a precursor to the full civil rights movement of the 1960s. Yet, incredibly, not one of us perceived the class and racial bias in what we were doing. Weis is right; these teachers, me included, were not deliberately or consciously fostering inequality, but, nevertheless, the consequences of our behavior was to exacerbate the effects of social class on our students.

In retrospect, my second experience, a short-term conversion to life-adjustment education, is even more embarrassing. That it was a result of naiveté rather than conscious bias against the working class and minorities does not mollify my mortification. The summer following the tracking experience, I enrolled in a graduate educational administration course that used a textbook by Harl Douglas, one of the leaders of the life-adjustment education movement. Douglas and other life-adjustment educators argued that about 20 percent of high school students could benefit from a college preparatory curriculum and another 20 percent from vocational education; the rest needed a "basic living" curriculum to prepare them for the personal and social problems they would encounter in life (a fuller discussion of life-adjustment education is included later in this chapter). The professor, a true believer, presented life-adjustment education as a humanitarian effort to meet the real needs of the great mass of American youth. After the first class, in the words of the southern gospel hymn, I was almost persuaded. Following the class, my twenty-three-year-old self found an isolated seat in a University Center lounge and wrestled with my doubts, finally concluding in a wave of euphoria that Douglas was right—what could schools be for if not to prepare students for the actual problems they had as adolescents and adults? But of course the whole idea was permeated with class, race, and gender bias. An unexamined assumption was that youth should be trained to play their "proper" role in an unchanging racist and patriarchal society in which extremes of wealth were natural and fixed. Educators would inevitably place individual students in curriculums based on their family's position in society; a life-adjustment curriculum for the children of the privileged would be a college-preparatory curriculum. Poorer youth would have even more obstacles to using the school as a ladder of vertical mobility. Unfortunately, my teacher education program had not taught me to look for the ways schools encourage inequalities. I hope that a historical examination of the ways that class bias has operated in twentieth-century schools may provide a useful perspective for you in finding and combating inequities in your own work.

Historical Perspectives

Once upon a time, in song, stories, and plays, popular culture labeled the decade of the 1890s—the gay 90s. (Gay, of course, had quite a different connotation than it does a century later.) Popular culture creates its own reality; in the case of the 1890s it was a happy, carefree reality much at odds with historians' views of turn-of-the-century America. Actually, it was a time when the American dream of perpetual progress seemed to be turning into a grotesque nightmare. Turn-of-the-century America was a place of huge disparities in wealth. The "Captains of Industry" (or the "Robber Barons") were engaged in the often gaudy display of enormous wealth that gave the period its appellations–the Gilded Age and the Age of Excess among others. These business leaders made their enormous fortunes without government regulation of their cut-throat competition or restraint of their exploitation of natural resources. Vernon Louis Parrington called the governmental subsidization of their pursuit of their wealth "The Great Barbecue": the poor "had been put off with the giblets while the capitalists were consuming the turkey."[9]

For the poor, life in the cities was often tragic. In the tenements several families sometimes shared a single room, sleeping in shifts. A single water spigot for a block was sometimes the only source of water, and the stench of rooms and streets was only made bearable by people becoming accustomed to it. These sordid rooms in which people lived were also often workplaces where family members otherwise unemployed earned a bit by sewing piece goods or rolling cigars. Cheap calories for survival were available in the penny beer dives in the basements of tenements. Opium dens were a fixture of the urban landscape, cocaine was legal and widely used, and narcotics were often an ingredient of patent medicine for children. The social gospel Baptist minister, Walter Rauschenbusch, cried out in pain that he had ten-year-old girls in his Hell's Kitchen parish selling their bodies for a dime in order to eat.[10]

There seemed to be an epidemic of juvenile crime in urban American. New York City serves as an example. Historian of childhood Joseph M. Hawes found numerous examples in the nineteenth-century *New York Times*: "Nearly every day small boys commit highway robbery–usually by snatching the purses of ladies–in the streets of New York and Brooklyn." In 1890, *The Times* reported that two boys, seven and ten, were charged with stealing horses; it was the second time the ten-year-old had been arrested for the same crime. *The Times* also complained about juvenile gangs, "half-drunken, lazy, worthless vagabonds," shooting guns and sometimes terrorizing people in their homes.[11] Children were, of course, not committing crimes just in sin-ridden New York. Hawes begins his book on juvenile delinquency in nineteenth-century America with a chapter on Jesse Pomeroy, the notorious "Boy Fiend" of Boston, who tortured and murdered young children in the 1870s.[12] Alcoholism, drug addiction, sexual exploitation, and criminal behavior were part of the urban youth culture in the 1890s as well as in the 1990s.

Many in the working classes in the cities engaged in strikes and civil disorder that openly challenged capitalism "on a scale approaching, in the eyes of many contemporaries, a civil war."[13] Respectable people were often horrified at the possibilities of disorder as well as the manners, speech, looks, and smells of the new immigrants. A common response of "successful" persons in society, then and now, is to blame the victims of social and economic injustices for their suffering and poverty. Individual character defects such as laziness or drinking are responsible for failure; for the most prejudiced among us, whole culture groups suffer from a scarcity of intelligence and the motivation needed to succeed in a competitive society. Attitudes about national and racial characteristics that would be considered ignorant and mean-spirited in mainstream society today were accepted as "scientific" among social scientists in the early twentieth century. Edward A. Ross, a "liberal" sociologist of the time, wrote in a popular college textbook of the strength of native propensities:

> There is an imposing stock of facts that seem to prove that the Negro has a fiercer sex appetite than other men, that the Irishman has an uncommon taste for fighting, the Jew for money-making, the gypsy for wandering, the Levantine for lying, the Slav for anarchy, the Frenchman for gesticulation.[14]

Such prejudiced characteristics of nationalities (often referred to as "races") were also commonly found in stories in elementary school textbooks.[15]

For those who feared that their Anglo-American culture was imperiled, one solution was to prohibit the immigration of "inferior nationalities" to our shores. As Ross put it, "If we wish our civilization to be democratic . . . we should bar out stupid elements. . . . However amiable the dogma that at bottom one race is as good as another, it is not only unscientific but positively mischievous."[16] In 1921 and 1924 Congress passed laws that severely restricted the immigration of southern and eastern Europeans.

But, in the eyes of most native-born Americans, including teachers and school administrators, something had to be done about the millions of uncouth and unsavory immigrants with inferior cultures and dangerous ideas who were already here. There are uncomfortable parallels in our own time. In the 1992 presidential election some conservatives, particularly those on the religious right, talked of a cultural war against immorality and un-Americanism. A century earlier, conservative reformers "looked to a Protestant holy war against sin, idleness, atheism, popery, and subversion. With the aid of God's will, prayers, itinerant revivalist ministers, and the dollars and organizational genius of big business, evangelicals would drive the heathen back, save souls, eradicate poverty and vice, and restore godliness, self-reliance, order, and prosperity to the land."[17]

The public schools were to play a major role in this cultural war through Americanization programs. Schools would be the primary battlefield and the teaching of traditional "American" values the major weapon. The best-known educational historian of the early twentieth century, Ellwood Patterson Cubberley, explained what the responsibilities of the schools were: "to assimilate and amalgamate these people as a part of our American race, and to implant in their children, so far as can be done, the Anglo-Saxon conception of righteousness, law and order, popular government, and to awaken in them a reverence for our democratic institutions."[18] Cubberley was pleased with the way schools performed their important function, reporting in 1909 that "each year the child is coming to belong more and more to the state, and less and less to the parent."[19]

Children and their parents paid a high price for the success of the Americanization program as reformers tried to reduce social conflict with school programs. "The public school as agent of the dominant culture was often unfeeling and heavy-handed in dealing with cultural conflicts," according to Stephen

E. Brumberg, historian of the Jewish immigrants' experience with the New York City schools. He writes that "It frequently denigrated the home culture in the eyes of its students and served to exacerbate the painful gap that opened between immigrant parent and child."[20] An immigrant writer helps us feel the pain of children undergoing Americanization: "I can't live with the old world, and I'm too green for the new. I don't belong to those who gave me birth or to those with whom I was educated."[21]

Present concerns with multiculturalism, including the need for everyone to understand and appreciate the diversity of the American people as well as to give minority children a sense of place in school, were simply not issues a century ago: "To have tried to be anything other than an Americanizing agent for immigrant children would have been contrary to the logic and function of the public or common school, as it was then understood."[22] However, opponents of multiculturalism might do well to remember that the single-minded devotion to teaching a single, Anglo world view a century ago was not successful. Immigrant children alien in their parents' homes and out-of-place in public schools often found exciting relief in the street culture: "And then came our street existence, our sweet, lawless, personal, high-colored life, our vent to the disciplines, and confinements of other worlds."[23] Teachers were commonly warned that the youth culture of the street "was their primary enemy."[24] A century ago, students dropped out, flunked out, or were otherwise pushed out in droves. Most children failed to complete elementary school, and many poor and immigrant children attended school for five years or less.[25]

As contemptuous as school leaders were of the culture of immigrant children in 1900, the common school curriculum was not as overtly social-class biased as it was to become as the century progressed. Despite single-minded conditioning to Anglo-Saxon, Protestant views, there was some virtue in a single curriculum with common goals, in a belief that all children needed the same knowledge. However, Horace Mann's ideal that the common school was to be the great equalizer was to be replaced with the idea that schools should segregate children by sorting them according to their projected vocations.

Industrial Education and Class Bias

The creation of different curriculums—vocational and academic—was a great betrayal of the promise of American schools to foster equal opportunity. In the early years of the twentieth century, one of the most popular education "reforms" was the sorting of students into differentiated curriculums, depending on their projected futures. Democracy in education no longer meant common learnings but learnings most appropriate to the roles persons were to play in society—roles determined in large part by race, social class, and ethnic background.

Much as in the 1980s and 1990s, the cries for reform a century earlier came from business leaders concerned with productive workers rather than from educators. In his historical study of social class and schooling in Chicago, David John Hogan argues that much of the late-nineteenth-century impetus for industrial education came from the business community. Their interest was economic rather than education reform: they wanted "a steady supply of manual workers with appropriate industrial skills and habits."[26] In his study of Boston, Marvin Lazerson found similar perceptions: the "problem was productivity, and the role of the school was to prepare each child for more efficient production."[27] Much the same was heard throughout urban America, and, as will be discussed in chapter six, even in the education campaigns of the rural South of the time. The school was to serve America by training skilled industrial workers.

Sympathetic school leaders supported businessmen, giving the common argument that I often found among southern school leaders of the time: the traditional curriculum was aristocratic, or at least undemocratic, whereas industrial education was democratic, helping the majority of youth develop the practical skills and attitudes necessary to earn a living.[28] School administrators endorsed a factory metaphor for their work by seeing "themselves as the shapers of the raw material which, when emerging as finished products, fulfilled the needs of hierarchical and specialized society."[29] One of their major tasks, then, became sorting children into the proper type of education as early as possible.

Influenced by the immensely popular 1909 study, *Laggards in Our Schools*, educators concluded that many children fell behind or dropped out because they lacked the intellectual or emotional capacity to profit from the traditional academic curriculum.[30] To gain maximum benefit from school, children needed to be categorized as early as possible into an academic type or a pre-vocation type. Among the latter type were the "concrete–minded," "seriously retarded" (at the time, retarded commonly meant behind in grade level), "anti-book," "physically active," and "individualistic."[31] Educators then often failed to realize that their categorizations of children were based largely on the consequences of poverty; they still do.

Professional sorters or selectors in the form of guidance counselors were trained and then hired to "scientifically" categorize students. By 1910, there were enough of them to hold their first national convention. Boston illustrates the creation of vocational bureaucracies. Early in the century, according to Lazerson, Boston developed an elaborate program of vocational guidance in the public schools. School counselors were hired at both the elementary and high school levels, vocational guidance lectures were given in elementary schools (particularly in poor, inner-city schools), vocational libraries were established, and aptitude tests were made the basis or admission to high schools of commerce and practical arts.[32]

Another major elaboration of the sorting function of the public schools was the junior high school. It was created to begin early differentiation, sorting students into three curriculums: general, commercial, or industrial. The National Education Association department of superintendency gave official approval to the junior high movement in 1915, praising "the increasing tendency to establish beginning with the seventh grade, differentiated courses of study aimed more effectively to prepare the child for his probable future activities."[33] In his study of Chicago schools, John David Hogan titled one of his chapters, "The Triumph of Vocationalism." In the junior high schools of that city in the 1920s, he found over 60 percent of the girls and nearly 70 percent of the boys were enrolled in vocational curriculums, and that such students spent five times as much time in shop classes as did students in the academic curriculum. Shop courses for boys "included practical experiences in electrical, print, metal, and woodworking process." At the same time eleven-to-thirteen-year-old girls were preparing for their futures by operating electric sewing machines in the sewing rooms.[34]

In 1917, Congress proclaimed the triumph of vocationalism when it passed the first national vocational education act, the Smith-Hughes Act. With this act the federal government supported shop courses and technological education in local schools throughout the country. In the name of economic efficiency, the power of American business over the public school curriculum was nationalized.

Those who argue that the schools reproduce inequities point to the industrial education movement to support reproduction theory: "Industrial education has proved to be an ingenious way of providing universal secondary schooling without disturbing the shape of the social structure and without permitting excessive amounts of social mobility."[35]

Class Bias in Pioneering Sociological Studies

Sociological studies show that the public schools have been remarkably successful in sorting students according to social class. In 1922, George S. Counts published a pioneering study of urban schools across the country from Bridgeport, Connecticut, to Seattle, Washington. The most obvious class bias that he found was that youth of lower classes were usually not in high school at all. In Seattle, he found that whereas 17.4 percent of the high school aged children of business proprietors were in school, only 1 percent of the children of miners, lumber workers, and fishermen were.[36]

Although lower-class children were usually not in high school, he found that those who were followed a different curriculum from their wealthier peers. He used Bridgeport High School to examine the relationship between fathers' occupations and the high school curriculums followed by their daughters. The largest group in the college preparatory curriculum were the daughters of business proprietors (35.2 percent); none of the high school daughters of common labors were in college preparatory; and only 1.2 percent of the daughters of carpenters, masons, and others in the building occupations were in college preparatory. In St. Louis he found that almost 40 percent of the sons of common laborers who were enrolled in high school were in the vocational courses, whereas less than 5 percent of the sons of business proprietors were.[37]

Counts saw the issue as class bias, not academic ability. He suggested that it is probable that youths' experiences with high schools depend more on whether "they come from the homes of the influential and more fortunate classes" than on their native abilities.[38] A student is likely to be in high school, he wrote, "not necessarily because of any special promise, but possibly because he is the only child of fond and well-to-do parents or because he likes football."[39] Counts clearly saw what many of his contemporaries did not, that, in a class society, differentiated curriculums result in injustice: "Why should we provide at public expense these advanced educational opportunities for X because his father is a banker and practically deny them to Y because his father cleans the streets of the city?"[40] Counts also anticipated present-day critiques of the undemocratic nature of differentiated curriculums by warning that some "foreign educators" may fear masses of citizens who have "trained minds capable of self-direction and critical thought," but that such fears were justified only in an authoritarian society.[41]

In the decades that followed Counts' research, educational sociologists continued to document the social class bias in public schools. In a classic study published in 1949, W. Lloyd Warner and his associates examined class in "Jonesville," including the relationship between social class and school attendance. They found that while all of a random group of school-aged children from the upper and upper-middle class were in school, over 40 percent of the upper-lower and nearly 90 percent of the lower-lower class children had dropped out. The researchers concluded that there was a two-way relationship between social class and school attendance. The culture of children affected their views, causing them to tend to accept or to reject schooling. At the same time the culture of teachers and school administrators resulted in attitudes about the social class of youth that caused them to "act as attractive or repellent agents," keeping students in or forcing them out of school.[42]

In 1953, Warner published *American Life: Dream and Reality* which continued to explore social class issues and education, particularly the class values of teachers. He reviewed a significant study by Gardner and Davis that anticipated much of what we now know about academic tracking. Teachers were asked to divide children into groups based on academic ability. The researchers then compared the teachers' ratings with the social-class background of the students. Eighty-five percent of the upper and upper-middle class students were placed in the top academic group, but only 11 percent of lower-class students were given a high rating. A number of factors were involved. In some cases, as you might suspect, the researchers indicated that upper-class children were better prepared and more highly motivated. In other cases, the teachers mistook the "lower-class manners, behavior, and speech" of students for lack of academic ability. More disturbing, as revealed in interviews, some teachers placed students where they did, not because of their estimate of ability, but because of overt class biases: "it would not be right to place him scholastically in a section that was below his social station, because 'he would not be with his own kind and would be forced to go around with children that were not of his cultural level.'"[43]

The best-known study of class in America during the 1940s was August R. Hollingshead's *Elmtown's Youth.*[44] Hollingshead divided the population of "Elmtown" into five social classes, class I being the highest and class V the lowest, and analyzed the impact of class on the experience of public school students. First, he looked at curriculum. There were three courses of study in the high school: college preparatory, general, and commercial; enrollment in them was heavily social-class determined. As an example, nearly two-thirds of the students from classes I and II were in the college preparatory curriculum whereas only 9 percent of those from class IV and 4 percent from class V were in the prestigious curriculum. The students were well aware (they always are) of the class bias.[45] An "Elmtown" female senior expresses the prevailing view of the students in the document that follows.[46]

> If you take a college preparatory course, you're better than those who take a general course. Those who take a general course are neither here nor there. If you take a commercial course, you don't rate. It's a funny thing, those who take college preparatory set themselves up as better than the other kids. Those that take the college preparatory course run the place. I remember when I was a freshman, mother wanted me to take home economics, but I didn't want to. I knew I couldn't rate. You could take typing and shorthand and still rate, but if you took a straight commercial course, you couldn't rate. You see, you're rated by the teachers according to the course you take. They rate you in the first six weeks. The teachers type you in a small school and you're made in classes before you get there. College preparatory kids get good grades and the others take what's left. The teachers get together and talk, and if you are not in college preparatory you haven't got a chance.

Grades were also influenced by social class. The researchers divided the grades assigned into three groups: high, medium, and low. More than half of the I and II class students' grade averages were "high" and not one received a "low" average. On the other hand, nearly 25 percent of the class V students failed one or more courses; less than 3 percent of the class I and II students failed a course.[47]

One of the most interesting and revealing parts of Hollingshead's study was an examination of the class bias in "extracurricular" activities. Whether pupils participated at all was class determined: all of the class I and II students participated in some school activity as did 75.3 percent of the class III students. Participation dropped to 57.4 percent for class IV students and to 27 percent for Class V. More significant was an analysis of the class bias of each school club: sixty percent of the members of the Home Makers' Club was class IV females and 71 percent of the library club was of class III females whereas 60 percent of the French club was class II females. Again, the students, then and now, understand the class bias as it operates in their schools.[48] A class IV female described the system in "Elmtown" in the document below:[49]

> Frankly, for a lot of us there is nothing here but just going to classes, listening to the teacher, reciting, studying, and going home again. We are pushed out of things. There is a group of girls here who think they are higher than us. They look down on us. I won't mention any names, but they are a group of girls from the higher families. They have a club that is supposed to be outside of school, but it's really in the school. They go from one club to the other and hog all of the offices. They're in all the activities. They talk about what they're doing, what they're going to do, and they won't pay any attention to us. They snub us and they won't talk to us. Some of them will speak to us sometimes, but most of the time they just ignore us. I'd like to be in the school activities and the school plays, go to the dances, and things like that, but they make us feel like we're not wanted. I went to some of the activities when I first started high school. Last year, I was in the Home Makers' and the Cheer Club, but they ignored me. Now I'm not in anything. If we go to the high school dances, nobody will dance with us. They dance among themselves and have a good time and we're nobody. If we go to the football games, it's the same way. Those Cheer Club girls are supposed to sit together at a game and root, but they don't. They break up into little groups and, if you're not in one of the groups, you're left out of things.

Through different formal curriculums, hidden curriculums, and extracurricular activities, public schools were quite successful in reproducing class inequities in the early twentieth century. But many working class persons were conscious of these biases in the schools and resisted attempts to limit the futures of their children. Historian David Nasaw summarized the conflict between the educators and the working class:

> The more the educators–with the applause of the business community –moved to adjust the curriculum to their "requirements," the more they [working-class students] elected the traditional academic courses.

> High school to them meant Latin and algebra, not metal-working and sewing. . . . Both parents and children knew what they wanted—and that was to escape the workplaces the new programs were designed to prepare them for.[50]

Educators, in turn, were often contemptuous of parents who did not understand the "limitations" of their children. Lazerson wrote of the educators: "critiques of fantasy in education, the lack of realism among the poor and working class . . . the chastisement of manual laborers for looking wistfully to the professions as a possibility for their children."[51]

Successful resistance was uneven. As examples, Brumberg concludes that resistance to the vocational curriculum by Jewish immigrants in Boston was often successful. Whereas Hogan found that resistance in Chicago, led by organized labor which organized mass meetings, campaigned in the labor press, and pressured governing boards, was largely unsuccessful against an alliance of business and education leaders.[52]

Life-Adjustment Education

Life-adjustment education of the 1940s and early 1950s was the nadir of unconscious, or at least largely unconscious, class bias among teachers, school administrators, and professors of education. The movement is an excellent example of how, in the name of reform, well-meaning, liberal-minded educators produce policies and curriculums that exacerbate the inequities that exist in society. As I underwent my conversion to life-adjustment education in that University Center lounge, the idea that the movement represented an adjustment to life as it was, with its existing social injustices, simply did not occur to me. After all Harl Douglas' textbook, the professor of the class, and the other students did not raise the issue. It probably did not occur to any of them. You may think me too cynical when I tell you that I think that if a similar proposal were made today, it might be objected to on a number of grounds, but, in most education classrooms, its social class bias would not be one of them.

Life-adjustment education had its beginnings in the Vocational Education Division of the United States Office of Education. At a 1945 conference sponsored by the Vocational Education Division, Charles Prosser, a leading lobbyist for industrial education, offered a resolution that was unanimously adopted. The resolution proposed the formula for functional curriculums that became a chief article of faith in the movement: 20 percent of high school youth would benefit from vocational education, becoming skilled workers; 20 percent would benefit from the traditional academic curriculum, a preprofessional training preparing an elite for college; but the other 60 percent needed life-adjustment training. The United States Commissioner of Education was enthusiastic, meetings of educators were held around the country to endorse it, a Commission on Life-adjustment Education for Youth was created, and soon textbooks (such as the one by Harl Douglas that so inspired me with the gospel of life adjustment) were being widely adopted in teacher education classrooms. The goals of the movement as written by the Commission were arguably worthy: "to equip all American youth to live democratically with satisfaction to themselves and profit to society as home members, workers, and citizens."[53]

The life-adjustment education needed by the 60 percent of youth not being served by vocational education or by the "medieval misconceptions" of advocates of an academic curriculum was to meet their "real problems." An official of the Connecticut State Department of Education indicated some of these real problems of youth: "preparation for post-secondary education, preparation for work, doing an effective day's work in school, getting along well with other boys and girls, understanding parents, driving a motor car, using the English language, engaging in recreational activities," etc.[54] "Basic living" curriculums became popular in the early 1950s. As an example, the Canton (Illinois) High School program included "personality, etiquette, family living and vocations." The Battle Creek, Michigan, curriculum was built around personal issues such as "Basic Urges, Wants and Needs, and Making Friends and Keeping Them." In Billings High School, Montana, "School and Life Planning" and "Growth Toward Maturity" were required courses whereas "Boy-Girl Relationships" and "Preparation for Marriage" were electives.[55] Such offerings trivialized school curriculums and curbed the possibilities of using schools for intellectual development, social mobility, or critical examination of society.

The feebleness of the rationale for life-adjustment education became apparent when it was attacked in the early 1950s, first by intellectuals and then by the press and the public generally for its anti-intellectualism. Its supporters had no strong defense. Historian Lawrence Cremin argues that, at a time of increasing concern about conformity, the movement was "as much the victim of its own ill-chosen name as of the deeper attacks on its principles and practices."[56]

The death of life-adjustment education is sometimes blamed on Sputnik, the first artificial satellite which was launched by the Soviet Union in 1957. Americans who were used to thinking of themselves as first in everything important and desirable were devastated. As has so often happened in American history when there is a crisis, the responsible powerful business and government leaders quickly sought to evade responsibility for their failures–in this case not to make launching such a satellite a high priority–by blaming the public schools: Johnnie can't do physics but Ivan can. Or, as Herbert M. Kliebard put it: "While American schoolchildren were learning how to get along with their peers or how to bake a cherry pie . . . Soviet children were being steeped in the hard sciences and mathematics needed to win the technological race that had become the centerpiece of the Cold War."[57]

In historical retrospect, blaming the public schools for Sputnik was ludicrous; once the money was appropriated, the United States was able to have its own satellite orbiting the earth within eighteen months, hardly enough time to make a physicist of Johnnie. But if Sputnik did not kill life-adjustment education, it required a post-mortem on the movement. Unfortunately for social justice in America, the death of life-adjustment education was found to be desirable (perhaps a mercy killing) because it was deemed detrimental to winning the Cold War, not because it was class biased. (In the aftermath of Sputnik, in 1958, Congress passed the first major piece of federal financial support for education, the National Defense Education Act (NDEA).

The 1960s: An Interlude of Reform

In the 1960s, amidst all the confusion and fumbling and the sometimes utter (but necessary) stupidity that accompanies democracy at work, an egalitarian spirit was being translated into activity by people and policy by governments. The civil rights and women's movements helped create changes that proponents hoped and opponents feared was the beginning of a social revolution in America. It was the "Age of Aquarius," sang the Fifth Dimension; it was *The Greening of America* wrote Charles Reich.[58]

For a brief time, mitigating bias in schools and other institutions against minorities, women, and the working class seemed possible. In powerful prose, "romantic critics" of education, including teachers and former teachers, wrote best sellers, exposing the hopelessness of poor children in schools that were pedagogical slums—the savage inequalities of a generation ago.[59] The federal government created Head Start, Upward Bound, Chapter I and other war on poverty programs that offered the possibility of meliorating some of the worst inequities in schooling.

The 1960s were also a time when increasing numbers of Americans were celebrating pluralism rather than trying to eliminate it. Black is beautiful and Polish is sexy on buttons and bumper stickers were pop culture manifestations of fundamental changes in the way non-Anglo Americans viewed themselves. In colleges and universities Black Studies, American Indian, and ethnic studies programs were created, and, in many places the traditional Anglo-Eurocentric public school curriculum was expanded to include more of the cultures of the nation's peoples. In some places, policies were developed to give parents in local communities more influence in the education of their children, Native Americans gained much more control over Indian schools, and bilingual programs were supported by the federal government.

Some of us who are sympathetic to the educational changes of the 1960s and 1970s are prone to forget the problems that accompanied the counterculture to school and made it easy for conservatives to mount a counterattack in the 1980s. This is a topic on which other voices need to be heard. Gerald Grant in his biography of a high school, *The World We Created at Hamilton High,* reminds us of many of the abuses, even horrors, of an urban high school in the period.[60] The yearbooks of the 1970s "featured a grim portrayal of the violence in the school with photographs of barred windows and barbed wire, with police in helmets and riot gear lined up in front of the school."[61]

Grant describes a school in which the unwritten slogan was "let the student decide." Let the student decide what to study if anything, whether to go to class, or whether to use dope.[62] Peter Clark conducted research for his doctoral dissertation as a participant observer for a year at Hamilton High. Clark describes radios playing throughout the school day including in some classrooms, over three-fourths of the students skipping classes at least once a week, and nearly one-half of the students being habitual absentees. The worst fears of conservatives were realized in the conditions that Clark observes:

> Alcohol and drug use "were quite high. . . . The general pattern was for beer, fruit wines, or alcohol and fruit juice mixes to be kept in cars and drunk either in the parking lot or on trips away from school." There was open petting and kissing in the halls, and more intense "making out" by couples in cars in the parking lot. Stealing and destruction of school property had increased, and teachers suffered "aggressive verbal abuse"; but "obscene or immoral activity was never an issue which was officially talked about."[63]

Clark attended a student party of the counterculture "freaks" at which many of them used drugs and went in the nude. Mescaline, marijuana, and amphetamines were used regularly by the "freaks"; some took LSD and opiates. "A number smoked marijuana habitually between classes."[64] Some students disrupted commencement by hooting and rolling across the stage on skateboards for their diplomas.[65]

In part, Grant blamed an "aggressive sense of legal rights" by students and their parents for the failure of school officials to enforce rules. He describes weary teachers who were increasingly the objects of racial hatred and slurs and sometimes violence. "Teachers joked that corporal punishment was a relic of the past—except for students who beat up on them." Women teachers were often the victims of "sexually degrading comments."[66] Grant blames the loss of consensus among the faculty at Hamilton High. Younger teachers fresh from campus protests sometimes encouraged their counterculture students; some smoked marijuana with them.[67]

In the struggle for social justice in education, mistakes were made and progress was uneven; the changes in the 1960s represented only a beginning. But the reformers were never allowed to correct their mistakes and many programs never had opportunities to prove their worth. Conservatives aborted the reforms.

The Conservative Restoration

The context for the theme of "conservative restoration" is, of course, the counterculture of the 1960s. As the decade waned and Richard Nixon replaced Lyndon Johnson, middle-class and middle-aged Americans increasingly viewed the young with alarm: they were so unkempt and unruly. Many Americans feared that students were being radicalized to the point that some were doubting that material possessions were the foundation for a good life. Children even questioned their parents' plans for their futures in corporate America.

In 1971, President Nixon's U. S. Commissioner of Education, Sidney P. Marland, launched a new program to get schools and youth back on the right path—career education. It represented extremism of vocationalism in public schools. Although the term "vocational education" was avoided as it was pejorative in the minds of some parents and teachers, the curriculum was to be permeated with occupational themes. Study of "career clusters" would begin in elementary school to acquaint children with the world of work. All secondary school students would prepare for a particular occupation or higher education.[68]

Critics concerned with class bias objected. The sorting function of public schools again became paramount. In career education, vocational guidance became an integral part of the curriculum; students in all courses were to study occupations that related to the subject matter. At the same time that occupational education was exalted, the intellectual function of academic courses diminished. Critics objected that career education was a way to "dumb down" critical learning.

My own direct experience with career education was brief, if unhappy. It was spring break. I had just finished a writing project, and my wife and I had conned friends into taking care of the kids while we spent a few days in an isolated, mountain lodge. When we arrived, the place was full of people, almost all men, wandering around in "informal clothes"–khakis, with alligators on their shirts and tassels on their shoes. Most of them looked as if they would be more comfortable in coats and ties–a very bad sign. Except for a couple of rooms, the entire lodge, including the foyer and lounge (which were replete with tripods and flip charts) had been reserved for a conference on career education. Background noise for three days was a choir, singing the praises of career education. This was the only time I ever seriously considered the possibility that the powers of the universe had picked me out for special punishment. Career education was simply too dumb an idea to be sustained and was rather quickly allowed to quietly pass away.

The Back-to-Basics Campaign

Another much more successful attempt to re-establish traditional authority and curtail critical thinking in the early 1970s was the back-to-the-basics campaign. The media were manipulated into declaring an educational emergency because of low standardized test scores. Permissive teachers and the lack of attention to the "3 Rs" were the familiar culprits in this crisis. The solution was obvious: traditional teachers demanding more drill, more homework, and more and tougher discipline. The manipulation of standardized test scores to manufacture educational crises has been a common ploy of the political and religious right since mid-century. We are a society obsessed with keeping score; numbers are what count. Each time the president makes a speech, polls immediately tell us, within a margin of error of three to five points, if he is more trustworthy, or at least more popular, than a half-hour before. It is not enough that my University's football team, the Big Orange, wins (except when they play Alabama); to be really successful they need to win by fifty points. In education, the public and the press give far too much credence to standardized test scores. Major sociological studies by Christopher Jencks and James S. Coleman in the late 1960s and early 1970s verified what teachers have always known: the major determinant of a student's achievement in school is family income (traditionally, in our male-dominated society, the single most significant factor is the father's occupation).[69] Not doing well on standardized tests? Too bad, you should have had richer parents.

Lower standardized test scores in post-WW II America were primarily a result of changing demographics in the school population. In 1950, 34 percent of American adults had graduated from high school. By 1985, the figure had risen to 74 percent.[70] More children from the lower social classes with non-scholastic backgrounds were in school, and, as should have been expected, average test scores dropped.

We might have viewed the increasing number of youth in school as a significant achievement as well as a challenge to increase the funding for schools in poverty areas and to reduce the cultural bias in schools so that poor and minority children might develop higher literacy skills. Instead, the Reagan administration declared a literacy crisis and issued its infamous call to arms, *A Nation at Risk* in 1983: "If an unfriendly foreign power had attempted to impose on America the mediocre educational performance that exits today, we might well have viewed it an act of war. . . . We have even squandered the gains in student achievement made in the wake of the Sputnik challenge."[71] *A Nation at Risk* was a poor analysis of the state of American public schools, but it was good propaganda. The stated parallel with the educational "crisis" after Sputnik is instructive. As the American political and industrial establishment blamed schools for their failure to keep pace in the "space race" in the 1950s, they attempted to displace responsibility for their poor judgment in the international marketplace in the 1980s. American driveways filled with Hondas, Nissans, and Toyotas, not because teachers failed to teach children to read and figure, but because General Motors, Ford, and Chrysler designed and engineered incredibly bad cars. Corporate executives and their political allies were acting as bullies when they pointed fingers at children and their teachers for failures of American industry to compete successfully with other nations.

Ira Shor has written an important book on educational policy and practice in the 1970s and early 1980s entitled *Culture Wars: School and Society in the Conservative Restoration.*[72] He wrote that "the beauty of [the educational] explanation for the economic crisis was that school was the solution as well as the problem."[73] The "manufactured" literacy crisis supported a traditional crusade based on "back-to-the-basics, business culture, religions fundamentalism, and authoritarianism."[74] A "manipulated picture of mediocrity" compared test scores of American students with those of societies that sent a much more elite group to secondary school, resulting in, among other things, a "gung-ho admiration for the Japanese way of working and education. A traditional, authoritarian, far-away society was held up as a model."[75]

The "solutions" offered by the national administration for the educational crisis exacerbated the social class bias of American education. First, there was the sin of omission: the administration, tied to a conservative social agenda and a low-tax ideology, denied that savage inequalities in school finance were a major part of the problem. "You can't solve the problems of education by throwing money at them," was too often their response to schools in poverty areas that were starved for school resources, even such basics as textbooks for every child. Moreover the inequities in school finance sent, and send, a powerful message to children about who they are. "Plush environments and small classes for the wealthy let them know that they are the dominant class," Shor writes: "Conversely, shabby, crowded classrooms impose disrespect on lower-income students. They learn that they are the dominated sector of society. Squalor and indignity in school confer the message of disempowerment learned in the home."[76]

Second, the administration, under the dogmatic, articulate leadership of Secretary of Education William Bennett, demanded a return to the traditional male-dominated, Anglo-English core curriculum, including standard English, celebrationist (cleansed and uncritical) American history, and traditional "masterpieces" of English and American literature. Bilingualism, multiculturalism, and women and minority studies were attacked (often angrily) as the source of the educational crisis. This powerful endorsement of the traditional canon in schools had two major effects. The first was to reinforce social control as an aim of the curriculum: good Americans were accepting rather than questioning or critical of their heritage, and true Americans descended from a single Anglo-European, Protestant cultural tradition. The second effect was to increase the advantages in schools of privileged, upper-income children. The value of their cultural capital, including their use of standard English, was enhanced. The valued and taught culture was their culture.

The leaders of the Conservative Restoration in education embraced enthusiastically the use of computers in schools. They implied that computer-assisted or computer-managed instruction would foster student learning by supplementing (or supplanting) teachers who were either inadequate or who were prone to stray from the ideology of officially sanctioned curriculum. (Unless critically minded teachers are careful, computers may be used as another way of trying to "teacher-proof" schools.) In addition, the conservative reformers with human capital goals for schooling insisted that widespread computer literacy was essential to success in the new high-tech job market. Shor argues persuasively that "if computer literacy is the new coin of the realm," richer kids will be more educationally privileged again and poor children will be even more disadvantaged. Wealthier students already have personal computers in their homes; use of computers like use of standard English is already part of their cultural capital. And to make matters worse, schools in wealthy communities will have more computers and more sophisticated hardware and software.[77]

Conclusion

As I write this chapter, U. S. Secretary of Education Richard Riley has released a five-year study of literacy in America that indicates that almost half of adult Americans have inadequate literacy skills to perform commonplace tasks. As usual, the political and religious right is using the findings to condemn public schools and their teachers. "From a high of 98 percent early in this century," conservative columnist Cal Thomas laments, "we have steadily declined to where there are nearly 50 percent illiterate or barely literate citizens." The reason for this disastrous decline in literacy that leads to crime and other social problems, according to Thomas, is that teachers stopped using phonics to teach reading. When phonics was used, elementary readers used Sir Walter Scott, William Shakespeare, Henry Thoreau, and other classic writers. Students could read these authors "because they were taught properly." And why don't teachers use phonics? It's simple: "government schools" would rather "appropriate billions more in tax dollars" than use an inexpensive method that works.[78]

Thomas' analysis is poppycock. It is based on an incredibly faulty statistic—that 98 percent of adult Americans were literate early in this century. If he has a source for his statistic, he doesn't cite it. Until recently, writers relied on self-reported literacy rates (census takers asked citizens if they could read) or years of schooling as evidence of literacy. Then and now, such data do not verify literacy. Early in this century, millions of Americans were functionally illiterate, including a high percentage of African-Americans, Native American, and Mexican-Americans who suffered from schools that were often even more inadequate than today's.

The leading historian of literacy in American, Carl Kaestle, writes that we are at much the same place we were in the 1920s *but at a higher level of literacy*:

> In the 1920s, just when Americans thought they had gotten some control over rudimentary literacy rates, limiting immigration and improving the reach of public schooling, particularly in the South, testing experts began to warn that among the nominally literate were far too many who could not use their literacy. . . . And when the 1930 census reported low outright illiteracy figures, the reading expert William Gray reminded educators that there were millions "who have learned to engage in the very simplest reading and writing activities but have not attained functioning literacy."[79]

American preoccupation with standardized test scores is troublesome for several reasons: it fosters teaching to the test, particularly with subject matter achievement tests; it encourages a belief that there is a body of knowledge (inevitably privileged knowledge) that all should master; and test results, as commonly reported, conceal as much as they reveal. One of the findings of standardized test scores unnoticed by the rightist critics of public schools and rarely noticed by the press is that standardized test results are a reflection of poverty in America. Except for South Africa, no other industrialized nation allows so many of its children to live in poverty, suffering from lack of such basics as food and medical care. Unlike other industrialized nations, we have two systems of schooling: one for the affluent and one for the poor. The schools for the wealthy and middle classes compete successfully with those of other nations; we suffer in international comparisons only if we include children who go to schools with "savage inequalities." As an example, the top 20 percent of our students have higher standardized test scores than their counterparts in Japan, and our top half do as well as their top half.[80] Much of the public outcry by the rich and powerful about standardized scores is just posturing–blaming teachers, students, and, unconscionably, the poor. The political and economic elites don't care about schools for the poor, not really. If they did, they would stop proposing false panaceas that would aid primarily the advantaged such as vouchers, and they would work instead to remove the savage inequities.

Public school educators are, of course, not blameless. The tragic fact is that public school educators too often have lacked faith in the ability of poor children and immigrant and minority children to develop intellectually or, perhaps worse, to need the skills and knowledge that result from academic training. Part of the problem is an incredible confusion about the purposes of the liberal arts and sciences, symbolized by school officials referring to them as college preparatory or, more likely, college prep. Rather than pre-college preparation, academic subjects should be considered sources of power, particularly for the poor. These disciplines when properly taught give youth an opportunity to struggle in more sophisticated ways with the human dilemmas they really care about, including their own place in American society; to experience in vicarious and safer ways human feelings of rage, lust, powerlessness, despair, etc.; and to develop the liberating skills of speaking, writing, and reasoning. I like Ira Shor's telling comment: "It is hard to find examples in education history of people being kept in their place with liberal arts."[81] Please notice that these purposes of a liberal arts education may be as easily achieved with a multicultural curriculum as with the traditional Anglo-American canon.

Poor and minority students also share responsibility for their school failures. They often resist the alien culture of the school with a "lived culture" of their own. The formal and hidden curriculums of the school are subverted by "silence, disruption, non-performance, cheating, lateness, absence, vandalism, etc."[82] In the lived culture of many of these students, school is a place to hang out, smoke a joint, score some sex. Resistance to the official culture of schools with their palpable smell of poverty, alien curriculums, boring routines, and fixation with order is understandable, perhaps even sensible—but it may also be extremely costly. Resistance by working-class students may cost them the possibility of using school for their own liberation. The cliché—education is power—is true or, at least, potentially true. Teachers have to help create schools where it is actually true.

Notes

1 Richard Henry Tawney, *Equality* (G. Allen & Unwin, 1931). Quoted in Paul Fussell, *Class: A Guide Through the American Status System* (New York: Summit Books, 1983), p. 15.

2 Sally Reed and R. Craig Sautter, "Children of Poverty: The Status of 12 Million Young Americans," Kappan Special Report, *Phi Delta Kappa*, June, 1990; "America in the 21st Century: A Demographic Overview," Population Reference Bureau, Inc., May, 1989; Jonathan Kozol, "The New Untouchables," *Newsweek*, Special Issue, (Winter/Spring 1990).

3 Jonathan Kozol, *Savage Inequalities: Children in America's Schools* (New York: Crown Publishers, 1991), p. 36.

4 *Ibid*, p. 159.

5 *Ibid*, p. 236; "TEA Statistics for 1991-92," Tennessee Education Association.

6 Theodore Sizer, *Horace's Compromise: The Dilemma of the American High School* (Boston: Houghton Mifflin, 1984), p. 6.

7 Lois Weis, "Inequality: A Sociological Perspective in Teacher Education," *Educational Foundations*, 1 (Fall 1986).

8 *Ibid.*, p. 42.

9 Vernon Louis Parrington, *Main Currents in American Thought* (New York: Harcourt, Brace and Company, 1927) Vol III, p. 27; Ray Ginger, *Age of Excess* (New York: The Macmillan Co., 1965).

10 Jacob Riis, *How the Other Half Lives: Studies Among the Tenements of New York* (New York: Charles Scribner's Sons, 1890); Eric F. Goldman, *Rendezvous With Destiny: A History of Modern American Reform* (New York: Alfred A. Knopf, Publisher, 1952); Walter Rauschenbush, *Christianity and the Social Crisis* (New York: The Macmillan Company, 1908).

11 J. Hawes, *Children in Urban Society: Juvenile Delinquency in Nineteenth-Century America* (New York: Oxford University Press, 1971), pp. 130-31.

12 *Ibid.*; Clinton B. Allison, "Students Under Suspicion: Do Students Misbehave More Than They Used To," *13 Questions: Reframing Education's Conversation*, eds. Joe L. Kincheloe and Shirley R. Seinberg, (New York: Peter Lang, 1992).

13 David John Hogan, *Class and Reform: School and Society in Chicago, 1880-1930* (Philadelphia: University of Pennsylvania Press, 1985), p. 5.

14 Edward Alsworth Ross, *Principles of Sociology* (New York: The Century Co., 1925), p. 60.

15 For numerous examples, see Ruth Elson, *Guardians of Tradition* (Lincoln: University of Nebraska Press, 1964).

16 Ross, p. 66.

17 Hogan, p. 12.

18 Quoted in Lawrence A. Cremin, *The Transformation of the School: Progressivism in American Education, 1876-1957* (New York: Alfred A. Knopf, 1961), p. 68.

19 Quoted in Stephan E. Brumberg, *Going to America Going to School: The Jewish Immigrant Public School Encounter in Turn-of-the Century New York City* (New York: Praeger Publishers, 1986), p. 201.

20 *Ibid.*, p. 208.

21 Anzia Yezierska, *Children of Loneliness*. Quoted in Brumberg, p. 118.

22 Brumberg, p. 208.

23 Samuel Ornitaz, *Haunch, Paunch, and Jowl*. Quoted in Brumberg, p. 78.

24 Marvin Lazerson, *Origins of the Urban School: Public Education in Massachusetts, 1870-1915* (Cambridge, MA: Harvard University Press, 1971), p. 247.

25 Lazerson; Colin Greer, *The Great School Legend* (New York: The Viking Press, 1973).

26 Hogan, p. 154.

27 Lazerson, p. 245.

28 Hogan, p. 155; see also Clinton B. Allison, "The Conference for Education in the South: An Exercise in *Noblesse Oblige*," *Journal of Thought*, 16 (Summer, 1981).

29 Lazerson, p. 257.

30 Leonard Ayres, *Laggards in Our Schools*, (New York: Russell Sage Foundation, 1909).

31 Lazerson, p. 183.

32 Henry J. Perkinson, *The Imperfect Panacea: American Faith in Education 1865-1990* (New York: McGraw-Hill, 1991), p. 147; Lazerson, pp. 191-193.

33 Quoted in Perkinson, p. 147.

34 Hogan, p. 191.

35 Michael B. Katz, *Class, Bureaucracy and Schools: The Illusion of Educational Change in America* (New York: Praeger Publishers, 1975), p. 123.

36 George Sylvester Counts, *The Selective Character of American Secondary Education* (Chicago, The University of Chicago, 1922), p. 47.

37 *Ibid.*, pp. 58 and 67.

38 *Ibid.*, p. 154.

39 *Ibid.*, p. 156.

40 *Ibid.*

41 *Ibid.*, p. 153.

42 W. Lloyd Warner and Associates, *Democracy in Jonesville* (Harper and Bros., 1949) excerpted in William O. Stanley et al., *Social Foundations of Education* (New York: The Dryden Press, 1956), pp. 237-238.

43 W. Lloyd Warner, *American Life: Dream and Reality* (Chicago: University of Chicago Press, 1953). Excerpted in Stanley, pp. 250-252.

44 A. B. Hollingshead, *Elmtown's Youth: The Impact of Social Classes on Adolescents* (New York: Science Editions, 1967 [1949]).

45 *Ibid.*, p. 168.

46 *Ibid.*, pp. 169-170.

47 *Ibid.* pp. 172-174.

48 *Ibid.*, pp. 201-202.

49 *Ibid.*, pp. 202-203.

50 David Nasaw, *Schooled to Order: A Social History of Public Schooling in the United States* (New York, Oxford University Press, 1979), p. 131. Quoted in Ira Shor, *Culture Wars: School and Society in the Conservative Restoration, 1869-1984* (Routledge & Kegan Paul, 1986), p. 45.

51 Lazerson, p. 201.

52 Brumberg; Hogan.

53 Quoted in Cremin, p. 336; Herbert M. Kliebard, *The Struggle for the American Curriculum, 1893-1958* (New York: Routledge, 1986).

54 Quoted in Kliebard, p. 253.

55 Kliebard, pp. 255-256.

56 Cremin, p. 338.

57 Kliebard, p. 265.

58 Charles A. Reich, *The Greening of America* (New York: Random House, 1970).

59 Among the books by "romantic critics" were James Herndon, *The Way it Spozed to Be* (New York: Simon and Schuster, 1968); Herbert Kohl, *36 Children* (New York: New American Library, 1967); Jonathan Kozol, *Death at an Early Age* (New York: Houghton Mifflin, 1969); George Leonard, *Education and Ecstasy* (New York: Delacorte Press, 1968); Neil Postman and Charles Weingartner, *Teaching as a Subversive Activity* (New York: Delacorte Press, 1969).

60 Gerald Grant, *The World We Created at Hamilton High* (Cambridge: Harvard University Press, 1988).

61 *Ibid*, p. 47.

62 *Ibid.*, p. 65.

63 *Ibid.*, p. 58.

64 *Ibid.*, p. 60.

65 *Ibid.*, p. 74.

66 *Ibid.*, pp. 54-64.

67 *Ibid.*, p. 150.

68 Shor; Joel Spring, *The Sorting Machine Revised: National Educational Policy Since 1945* (New York: Longman, 1989).

69 James S. Coleman, *Equality of Educational Opportunity* (Office of Education, Washington D, C., 1966); Christopher Jencks et al., *Inequality* (New York: Basic Books, 1972).

70 Lawrence A. Cremin, *Popular Education and its Discontents* (New York: Harper and Row, 1989), p. 1.

71 *A Nation at Risk: The Imperative for Educational Reform*, The National Commission on Excellence in Education (Washington, DC, 1983).

72 Shor.

73 *Ibid.*, p. 164.

74 *Ibid.*, p. 64.

75 *Ibid.*, p. 126.

76 *Ibid.*, p. 168.

77 *Ibid.*, pp. 133-135; see also Larry Cuban, *Teachers and Machines: The Classroom Use of Technology Since 1920* (New York: Teachers College Press, 1986).

78 Cal Thomas, Syndicated Column, "Illiteracy is Growing, Dangerous Affliction," *Knoxville News-Sentinel*, September 16, 1993.

79 Carl F. Kaestle, "Literacy and Diversity: Themes from A Social History of the American Reading Public," *History of Education Quarterly*, 28 (Winter 1988) p. 548. See Kaestle's study: *Literacy in the United States: Readers and Reading Since 1880* (New Haven: Yale University Press, 1991).

80 Ian Westbury, reported in William Raspberry, "Underrating Our Schools," *Knoxville News-Sentinel*, October 12, 1993. Much more research data on international comparisons of educational achievement may be found in David Berliner's forthcoming book, *The Manufactured Crisis*.

81 Shor, p. 50.

82 *Ibid.*, p. 183.

VI

African-Americans and Education: Do Schools Reproduce Racial Bias in America?

Yesterday, after writing for a few hours on this chapter, I listened to a radio talk show on the way to campus to teach a history of education class. (Such listening is an incredibly unhealthy preparation for teaching; it fills the brain with balderdash and the stomach with acid.) The topic was ethnic cleansing in Serbia and Bosnia. A caller waxed eloquently on the moral superiority of America. We may have our faults; we aren't perfect, he said, but we have never engaged in that kind of behavior. The talk show host affirmed rather than contradicted this nonsense. The failure to face reality is commonplace among Americans. We in white society engage in a pathological denial of our racism. We suppress recognition that the treatment accorded generations of American Indians by white Americans *was* ethnic cleansing and that the treatment of the African-Americans through much of the twentieth century was as racist as the recent apartheid system in South Africa. To repress is to not take responsibility, to avoid, or to distort reality. Repression of past racism in American education distorts the present and makes it difficult for teachers to do good work in a multi-racial society.[1]

Because of the dominance of power by whites and residential segregation, many Americans do not understand how multiracial our society is and how racially diverse it will become in the near future. By 2010, nearly 40 percent of persons living in America under age 18 will be of African, Asian, Native American,* or Latino descent. Members of these minorities are among the poorest of Americans. Racial and ethnic minorities are about two-and-one-half times as likely to live in poverty as other American families. About 45 percent of African-American children and nearly 40 percent of Latino children are living in poverty. And approximately 40 percent of American Indians and Latinos and 25 percent of African-Americans will drop out of schools.[2]

Elites often propose education as the remedy for poverty and other social ills. For most members of minorities, however, education has and continues to be an imperfect panacea.[3] For one thing, those who stay in school will experience the same failures of schools that I discussed in chapter five. As indicated before, part of the problem is money. More funds are spent on schools for elite white children who don't have the desperate need for quality schooling in order to succeed in the majority culture as do minority children. Part of the problem is curricular. Schools reflect the cultural capital of elite whites; they are likely to feel at home there. For many minority students, however, experiencing the culture of the public school is like going to a foreign country. When a person doesn't understand the formal language very well and can't identify the landmarks, it's difficult to get anywhere. As long as schools mirror upper-middle-class white culture, minority children need more help in making progress; they generally receive less.

Another part of the problem is that the unstated purpose of schooling is often social control rather than social mobility. Much emphasis is placed on learning to obey the rules and respecting authority, sometimes more than on learning academics. In often-unconscious racism, school personnel place minorities in vocational rather than in academic programs. And, in what is probably the most systematic racist policy in public schools today, minorities are placed in lower academic tracks in secondary schools. Tracking is often a way of racially

*American Indian, rather than Native American, is still the term preferred by many members of Indian nations and by American Indian scholars.

segregating students in schools that are ostensibly desegregated.[4]

In his social foundations of education textbook, Joel Spring discusses a highly publicized case that exemplifies the frequent relationship between academic tracking and racism. In Selma, Alabama (infamous locale of violent conflict during the civil rights movement of the 1960s), a dispute about tracking in 1990 made national headlines. In Selma, students' placement in academic tracks was based primarily on teachers' recommendations. Ninety percent of white students were placed in the top two tracks: college preparatory and advanced placement. Only 3 percent of African-American students were in the top two tracks even though many black students had standardized test scores as high as white students who had been placed in the higher tracks. Selma's African-American superintendent of schools, Norward Roussell, attempted to achieve some racial fairness by increasing the percentage of black students in the top two tracks to 10 percent. The white-dominated school board fired him. He was reinstated only after a boycott by African-American students and adverse national publicity.[5]

The racial bias in Selma was profound, if commonplace. But the dimensions of the injustice cannot be understood adequately except in historical context. The African-American experience in schooling provides numerous examples of reproduction theory. Reproduction theory, you will remember, propounds the idea that inequities in society are systematically (some would say deliberately) reproduced in schools. Throughout the history of African-American schooling in America, the kind of curriculum that leads to economic and social success has been systematically and often deliberately denied to black children.

Reproduction theory should be balanced with resistance theory. Despite the rhetoric of the powerful: "It is an appropriate education for your abilities" or "It is an education to prepare you for your future life," or (as a last resort of those who cannot find any other justification for imposing an inferior curriculum on minorities) "It is the only kind of education that is politically feasible." Those who are being discriminated against often (eventually, almost always) understand that they are being offered an inferior education to that being received by the children of elites. And the less powerful resist the imposition of an inferior kind of education, overtly if possible, covertly if not.

Educational histories of several minority groups in America provide numerous examples of attempts to use schools to reproduce inequalities as well as illustrations of resistance of minorities to racist school policies. Trusting that one topic treated in some depth rather than a number of topics treated superficially will provide a better context for understanding the nature of racism in American education, I will concentrate on the African-American experience from slavery to the end of legal requirements for segregated schools.

Historical Perspectives

Education During Slavery

Some of you may be surprised at a discussion of African-American education during the period of slavery. But education is, of course, much broader than schooling. In 1960, historian Barnard Bailyn offered what has become a classic definition of education: "not only . . . formal pedagogy but the entire process by which a culture transmits itself across the generations."[6] Some historians think that this definition is too broad and prefer that the definition be limited to processes of teaching skills and values that are deliberate, systematic, and sustained.[7] Others are concerned that definitions should include the idea that education is an active process and should emphasize that which is learned, not just what is taught. Regardless of definitions, African-Americans were certainly educated during the era of slavery, as are all people who live in human society, even under the grimmest of circumstances.

Reproduction theory may be used to help explain the education of slaves on the plantations of the American South. Planters used education in attempts to convince African-Americans, critics of slavery, and (perhaps most importantly) the planter class itself that black people were natural slaves. If Africans were convinced that slavery was in the natural order of things and that God had intended them to be slaves, they should, the supporters of slavery hoped, accept their lot. And slave owners could more easily justify the peculiar institution of slavery if slaves were thought to be sub-human. For if they were fully human, slave owners were evil, and there are few things that are more self-destructive than the recognition, or the belief, that one is evil. The mental health of slave owners then required that slavery have justification beyond its potential profitability. There was always Christianity, of course. Apologists for slavery had long argued that for Africans, who would otherwise have died as pagans, a few decades of physical slavery in this world was a small price to pay for an eternity in paradise. Many Southerners were still justifying slavery on this basis in the twentieth century: "May [slave owners] rest in peace, for they earned it, and never got any credit for their labors" for their patience, industry, and Christianity "had metamorphosed African cannibals into useful men and women."[8]

But a belief that Africans were different, and inferior, to Europeans had an even more universal appeal than saving souls. Popular prejudices as well as more sophisticated "scientific evidence" created an elaborate doctrine of racial inferiority. As an example, Dr. William Cartwright of the University of Louisiana was one of a number of prestigious scholars in the ante-bellum South, who gave "scientific" credence to racism. Cartwright testified in court and assured readers of southern literary magazines that Africans were physiologically different from whites. Slavery was good for Africans, he insisted, because, when left alone, they tended to be inert, and physical labor exercised their organs and prolonged their lives.[9] The will to believe in the racial inferiority of black people was strong, and many white Americans held their racist views sincerely–another illustration of why sincerity is only a minor virtue.

Planter education for slaves, then, had two major goals: to teach skills to make the institution profitable and to teach values to make African-Americans appear sub-human. Slaves learned numerous skills, particularly job skills. Although most slaves were field hands or household servants, there were few occupations of the 18th and 19th centuries to which some slaves were not assigned: baker, barber, bookkeeper, butler, mason, manager, nanny, nurse.

But most slaves were limited to a circumscribed education with the goal of producing the sub-humans the defenders of slavery insisted that African-Americans naturally were. In his classic (and controversial) study of slavery, conveniently titled *Slavery*, Stanley Elkins' thesis is that planters were engaged in attempts at infantile regression, of deliberately making a child-like race, of producing "Sambo."[10] Sambo (a pejorative term) has the traits and characteristics of racists' stereotypical African-Americans: childish, lazy, shiftless, irresponsible, docile, superstitious, dimwitted, but happy. According to this theory of infantile regression, slaves learned, often under the duress of the whip, to exhibit these characteristics to white folks. A self-assured, intelligent-behaving African was a threat to the doctrine of racial inferiority and, thus, to the institution of slavery. Our history remains with us; we should not be surprised at the threat to basic beliefs that causes a racist to see competent African-Americans as "uppity."

Illiteracy of slaves was a major pillar of the doctrine of racial inferiority, and the circumscribed education disallowed teaching slaves to read. Much more basic than the fear that slave literacy might make slave rebellions easier to organize or abolitionist literature more widely available was the understanding that illiteracy both symbolized and safeguarded the image of Africans as sub-human. It was much easier to argue that Africans were incapable of higher intellectual functioning if they were not allowed to learn to read. South Carolina passed a law in 1740 making it illegal to teach a slave to read, and a number of other southern colonies (and later states) passed similar laws. But even where formal laws were not enacted, teaching slaves to read was against the mores and folkways of the society—often more powerful forces for controlling behavior than statutes.

Even when Africans appeared to be able to read English, racists argued, they had simply memorized words and were incapable of higher intellectual functioning. An example is Senator John C. Calhoun of South Carolina, the South's most famous proponent of slavery, who is said to have declared that no African could learn Latin, and if he ever met a black person who knew Latin he might reconsider his estimate of African intelligence. Since Africans were not allowed to learn the classical languages, his prejudices were deceptively easy to sustain.

A basic source of optimism for human freedom is that many of us simply never give up struggles to escape from those who attempt to control us. As some of my Appalachian neighbors say, we are just too blamed cussed to do what someone else wants us to do. When persons recognize that they are being controlled in the social, political, or economic interests of other groups, some will find ways to attempt escape from their assigned or circumscribed condition. Some post-modern theorists call the efforts of non-elites to thwart the power of elites to control them "resistance." In the face of the opposing forces of slavery, for even small numbers of African-Americans to resist by learning to read is testimony to the power of human agency.

Hidden Passages

In his prize-winning history of the African-American educational experience, Henry Allen Bullock calls ways that slaves learned to read hidden passages.[11] Knowledge about how slaves became literate comes from many sources: memoirs, diaries, autobiographies, journals, and stories handed down from generation to generation. A major source of information is the depression-era Federal Writers Project, a New Deal agency that, among other activities, hired out-of-work scholars to interview former slaves. These sources indicate that slaves learned to read in a variety of ways. The most common seemed to be children teaching other children, often by playing school. An innocent game turned out to be surprisingly subversive. Schools, of course, involve significant power deferentials with teachers possessing ascribed power over children. On plantations, white children had the ascribed position by virtue of caste and because they had experience with schooling. Slave children were obviously a source of docile students. In most cases, it is likely that white children were just enjoying the exercise of power by playing teacher rather than deliberately attempting to undermine one of the pillars of slavery—black illiteracy. But literacy was a real danger to perceptions of African sub-human status. Some of you will remember the incident in Alex Haley's *Roots* when the plantation owner sold a slave girl to remove her from the plantation and to punish his daughter who had taught her black friend to read.

In incredibly difficult undertakings, slaves sometimes took responsibility for their own literacy. They learned on their own from stolen primers or they bribed poor white children in the vicinity with pilfered food. But the penalty for slaves teaching others to read was sometimes death. Scipio, a slave, "was put to death for teaching a slave child how to read and spell, and the child was severely beaten to make him 'forget what he had learned.'"[12] Black preachers were (and still often are) a powerful source of resistance to the degraded conditions of their people. African ministers who could read the scriptures were not only themselves a visible contradiction to the doctrine that blacks were sub-human; they were also a source of reading teachers for others. Planters who justified slavery, in part, on the saving of Africans' souls found it difficult logically to prohibit the work of Christian preachers among them, although some planters, being above law and logic, did just that. Others would not allow black preachers who could read on the plantation, allowing only those who had memorized scriptures from frequent hearing. They were said to know the "word" rather than being able to read the "word." Other slave owners encouraged or insisted on slaves attending the planters' church, sitting separately of course, often in the balcony. Here they were protected from the subversive influences of the African preachers and could be inculcated with a theology supporting slavery.

White ministers were a hidden passage to African literacy as well. Throughout American history, the Christian clergy has included the most reactionary upholders of the status quo as well as the most radical agents of social change. The religious right on one hand and liberation theology on the other are only current manifestations of these poles. Some ministers in most Christian denominations resisted the conventional wisdom by teaching slaves. Quakers were a particular problem for true believers in the doctrine of racial inferiority. Their "peculiar" ideas about peace and the "brotherhood" of humans made them particularly troublesome to the military-loving, racist southern elite.

One of the most interesting and devastating challenges to the doctrine of racial inferiority was conducted by a group of prominent Presbyterians who directly challenged John C. Calhoun's assertion that an African could not learn Latin, the curriculum of the elite. Although there is some historical controversy about the details of the story, according to southern historian Edgar Wallace Knight, the white Presbyterians selected a young "full-blooded" African, John Chavis. They tutored him in the classical languages and sent him to Princeton College where he was an outstanding student. Chavis returned to his native North Carolina and opened a well-known classical school. Since he could not teach black children, his students were white, including many from prominent families who became political leaders in the state. He lost his school in 1831 when the North Carolina state legislature passed a law making it illegal for an African-American to teach.[13]

The planters themselves were sometimes hidden passages from a circumscribed education as some of them promoted literacy for a few of their slaves. African-American historian Bullock called these planters permissive because they, by indulging themselves and their slaves, were challenging a major rationale of the institution of slavery. They had a variety of motives. In some cases their goal was economic; in today's language, they were investing in human capital. Literate slaves could do work often done by white employees, less expensively and often more reliably. In other instances, literate slaves made the planter and his family's lives more convenient. A trusted literate slave, as an example, could be sent many miles to a town with a list of supplies to purchase, including newspapers and other reading materials.[14]

Other motives, including kinship and feelings of affection, were more complicated. Even in a social institution as perverted as slavery, persons living together sometimes developed deep emotional attachments which led slave owners to give special privileges to favorites, including tutoring or schooling. Manumission (freedom) was the greatest gift, and literacy sometimes made life as a freed person easier. Sometimes these "privileged" slaves were children or grandchildren of the slave owners. A British visitor to the large plantations of the old

South is supposed to have observed, in mock surprise, that it was remarkable how often the butler looked like the master of the house.

A major hidden passage for slaves to planter-controlled education was a competing system of education under the control of Africans themselves. Thomas L. Webber writes of this alternative education in *Deep Like the Rivers: Education in the Slave Quarter Community*. Webber indicates a number of reasons for the failure of racist white education among slaves. One that is often a problem for teachers is that the whites "made the mistake of assuming . . . that what they taught their slaves was what their slaves learned."[15]

He documents that white education's message of black inferiority "directly contradicted understandings, attitudes, values, and feelings which slaves learned from birth," and, perhaps most incredibly, he finds that whites were so sure of the subhuman status of Africans that they were unable to see that Africans had a culture that was being passed on from generation to generation.[16]

Education During Reconstruction

One of the best illustrations of the racism of American society is the historical treatment of the "reconstruction" of the South following the Civil War, or as Southerners still call it, the War Between the States. Through much of the twentieth century, the emphasis has been on the mistreatment of southern whites by northern Radical Republicans. The story was made familiar by films (beginning with the first modern full-length film, *The Birth of a Nation*), novels (including the perennial best seller, *Gone with the Wind)*, popular histories (one of the most popular and most damaging was Claude Bowers', *The Tragic Era*), and scholarly histories (often called the Dunning School after William Dunning of Columbia University). This racist interpretation of the period of reconstruction had a fascinating cast of characters: mean-spirited, money-hungry carpetbaggers coming from the North to prey on proud but defeated, poverty-stricken Southerners; contemptible scalawags, Southerners who Judas-like betrayed the "lost cause" and their own people by supporting the carpetbaggers; and ignorant, newly freed black people bent on drinking, looting, and raping. Southern historian C. Vann Woodward writes of "the consoling security of Reconstruction as the common historical grievance, the infallible mystique of unity," a myth which gave a separate identity to the South.[17] The traditional story was also used in attempts to justify terrorism, including that by the Ku Klux Klan and other vigilante groups, directed toward African-Americans for generations.

Black historians, notably W. E. B. DuBois, challenged this interpretation of reconstruction early in the twentieth century, and, beginning in the 1950s, specialists on reconstruction have fundamentally revised it. Unfortunately and incredibly, many teachers still teach the outdated, racist, traditional story.

Following the Civil War, reconstruction governments created public school systems in the South, and widespread schooling began for African-Americans. Despite these advances, until recently, historians of southern education were critical of the efforts of reconstruction officials, often African-American or northern whites, to provide for public schools. The best-known historian of southern education in the first half of the twentieth century, Edgar Wallace Knight, argued that, rather than helping, the reconstruction governments exacerbated the South's educational backwardness because they created distrust of governmental expenditures for public programs, including schools. They hurt the cause of education by giving public schools a Yankee taint.[18]

As a teaching ploy I sometimes describe the conditions of newly freed slaves: many disoriented by unknown futures, most landless in a rural area where they knew only farming, some hungry refugees. Would they, I ask, perceive schooling to be important or mainly irrelevant to their lives? Either having read their assignments or, more likely, being aware of my sneaky ways, most students respond that African-Americans viewed schooling with great enthusiasm. This was the case as a whole people from toddlers to their grandmothers seemed to be showing up at the schoolhouse door. Northern and foreign correspondents reported on the freed persons' enthusiasm for schooling as one of the great curiosities in the newly conquered South. As slaves they had been denied schooling, and their illiteracy was used to document their inferior status. They might not be able to get the rumored promise of forty acres and a mule, but the long-denied education that differentiated them from the white caste was within grasp. They shared in the general American faith in education. There was pathos in their faith—and tragedy in that their faith in education failed to live up to its promise.

Reconstruction was a time of great promise for the education of newly freed persons. Perhaps the most striking aspect of the educational history of the time was the degree to which African-Americans wished to control their schools. Throughout the South, African-Americans started schools on their own or through their churches or continued underground schools that had existed secretly in the ante-bellum urban South. In 1866, an educational official of the Freedmen's Bureau estimated that there were already 500 of these "native schools" in existence. This figure does not include several times that number of Sabbath schools in black churches that taught basic literacy as well as religion.[19]

In addition, missionary societies sent thousands of teachers from the North; these missionaries were among the detested carpetbaggers. Although most northern churches sent missionary-teachers to the freed persons, the largest group came under the auspices of the American Missionary Association of the Congregational Church, a denomination that had been a hotbed of abolitionists. Most of these teachers were young women who were motivated by a zeal to do good by securing the freedom of black people through schooling. Other motives for going to the exotic and dangerous South included a sense of adventure and, in some cases, a need to escape the control of fathers or other men in their lives.

Whites often coerced black parents who sent their children to missionary schools by refusing to employ them, evicting them from their houses, or with threats of violence if all else failed. (Similar tactics were used a century later to keep black parents from sending their children to formerly all-white schools under "freedom of choice" plans in the 1960s.) To protect African-Americans and their white supporters, including the missionary teachers, from hostile whites, Congress created the Bureau of Refugees, Freedmen, and Abandoned Lands, better known simply as the Freedmen's Bureau. Using missionary teachers, it created a rather complete school system, spending almost half of its budget on schools for African-Americans. By 1865, it had established nearly 600 schools that were often in competition with "native schools" established by African-Americans.

True believers in the superiority of Yankee institutions, missionary teachers were often atrocious anthropologists. Although historians have long commented on white Southerners' contempt for Yankee teachers, recent researchers have emphasized African-American distrust of these missionary teachers. Jacqueline Jones and Ronald E. Butchart have written excellent recent histories of the missionary teachers and the freedmen's schools.[20] In part, members of the black community simply wanted to operate their own schools and were more comfortable with black teachers who shared their culture. But, in addition, white missionary teachers too often approached the black community with an air of superiority, indicating that Africans were as yet little more than savages, inferior in morals and intellect. Multicultural educators today would be appalled by their behavior.

Yet, for the most part, schools taught by African-Americans and by northern missionaries offered a curriculum quite like that in northern white schools: reading, writing, spelling, and arithmetic at the elementary level; literary subjects at higher levels; and the classical course in black colleges. It was not a special curriculum for a subservient people. However, when federal troops were withdrawn and conservative southern whites returned to power at the end of the reconstruction era, an education to reproduce racial inequities was reestablished.

The Great Detour

After the infamous Compromise of 1877 that put a defeated presidential candidate in the White House, federal troops were withdrawn from the last three southern states, and conservative white control was restored in the South. African-Americans who had been subjected to intimidation and violence, especially when they attempted to use their political rights, were "legally" and formally subjugated. Poll taxes and biased literacy tests were passed in the southern states which nullified the black vote. The most famous and most blatantly discriminatory was the "Grandfather Clause," a 1898 Louisiana law that required a literacy test but exempted descendants of those entitled to vote before 1867. In the hands of local racist election officials who assessed literacy, it prevented even college-educated African-Americans from voting while allowing the most ignorant white man (women couldn't vote regardless of color) the ballot.

In the late nineteenth century, a policy of rigid racial segregation was being established, a policy commonly referred to as Jim Crow. C. Vann Woodward's *The Strange Career of Jim Crow* is a classic study of this policy of apartheid.[21] Jim Crow affected all aspects of life in the South. Georgia prohibited chaining white and black prisoners together on chain gangs, and New Orleans required separate red light districts for white and black prostitutes. A series of court decisions sanctioned racial segregation. The most far reaching was a case decided by the Supreme Court in 1896, Plessy *v.* Ferguson. Louisiana had passed a law requiring railroads to segregate the races in separate cars, seemingly a clear violation of the equal protection of the laws clause of the 14th Amendment. In an eight to one decision, however, the Supreme Court decided that states could require that public facilities be separate if they were equal. This "separate but equal" doctrine gave constitutional approval to state-mandated segregated public schools. In practice, schools in the South were certainly separate; they were rarely equal. In 1940, as an example, black public school students were receiving about one-third as many tax dollars as white students. In racist America, judges ignored differences in the quality of black and white schools, accepting the fiction that they were equal. Jim Crow is the context for examining ways in which southern elites in the early twentieth century attempted to limit African-Americans to an education that would reproduce inequalities.

Black leadership in this unhappy period for African-Americans may be symbolized by Booker T. Washington (1856-1915). Generations of children, black and white, have studied Booker T. Washington in school as the great leader of his race. Washington was one of the few African-Americans in the public school curriculum of the early twentieth century because, in racist America, he was an acceptable model of how a black person should behave. Washington was born a slave in an area that was soon to become West Virginia. Even for a slave he suffered excruciating poverty as a child, often being hungry. He had no eating utensils, no bed, no way to bathe. As has been true of many teachers born into lower social classes, he later overemphasized the importance of symbols of middle-class respectability. As an example, he called the toothbrush one of the major instruments of western civilization.

Young Washington became a servant to a "Yankee woman" who, admiring his diligence, encouraged him to go to school. He was admitted to Samuel Chapman Armstrong's Hampton Institute. The son of missionaries to the Hawaiian Islands, Armstrong thought he knew the kind of education that "primitive" people needed to prepare them for their lives–an industrial education. Armstrong thought labor was a spiritual force; laboring made a person more intelligent and honest. At Hampton, Washington learned his lessons well: the hope of his people lay in hard work and submission to authority.[22]

He was called to create a black normal and agricultural school at Tuskegee, Alabama, in 1881–a time when hundreds of African-Americans were being lynched annually. Here he practiced the philosophy of education that he hoped would reduce white opposition to black schooling. An important point needs to be made here: industrial education was designed more to teach a system of values, an ethic, rather than to produce skilled workers who could actually earn a living by practicing a trade. Young African-Americans might learn skilled trades, say carpentry or masonry, but except in African-American communities, the "color line" in the South required a division of labor: skilled, higher paid jobs for whites; nonskilled, poorly paid jobs for blacks. African-Americans worked on construction jobs, but they fetched and carried; they did not lay the bricks. Their agricultural education was also directed toward a nonexistent future. They might learn scientific agriculture, but in the crop-lien system of the time, African-American farmers were perpetually in debt to land owners, and they had little choice but to farm as they were told, planting cotton right up to the cabin door. Black farmers lived in peonage.

No longer under the duress of the whip as slaves, black workers were to have the values of hard work, regularity, punctuality, sobriety, and submission to authority instilled in them. From today's perspective, industrial education for African-Americans was directed toward producing a dependable, cheap, and docile labor force for the "ruling class." It was an education calculated to reproduce the inequities in the society.

Booker T. Washington did not see it that way. He argued that by producing good workers, industrial education would reduce white hostility toward black schooling and slowly lead to greater economic security and even prosperity for African-Americans. He insisted that as blacks became better educated and more prosperous, political rights, including the right to vote, would be returned to them. In the meantime, African-Americans should accept their inferior social status, be patient, and expect gradual improvement in future generations. In 1896, he was the only black person invited to address the Cotton States Exposition. He concluded his speech with the famous words: "In all things that are purely social we can be as separate as the fingers, yet one as the hand in all things essential to mutual progress." White America loved the words and the sentiment. He said what they wanted to hear from black America, and the white press and politicians dubbed him "the spokesman of his race."[23]

The Southern Educational Campaigns

At the beginning of the twentieth century, the southern states still didn't have public school systems, though they had been decreed by law. Public schools lacked popular and, as a result, financial support. In the rural South (and most of the region was rural), public schools were often little more than shacks, heated by fireplaces and taught by semi-literate teachers who frequently had but months of elementary schooling themselves, and these were the schools for white students. Where they existed, schools for African-American students were almost always worse. These conditions were a result of poverty, of cultural attitudes about schooling and public expenditures for social purposes, and, of most consequence for this chapter, of race.

In the first decade of the twentieth century, a gigantic propaganda campaign was launched to convert white Southerners to a faith in public school systems—the southern educational movement. The campaign was led by ministers (North and South) and southern educators and financed by northern "philanthropists"—captains of merchandising and industry. The leaders of the campaign were convinced that a major obstacle to the establishment of public school systems was opposition by white Southerners to schooling for African-Americans. They feared particularly that reactionary politicians would use the "race issue" to defeat legislation to raise taxes for education.

The leaders of the campaign, Northerners as well as Southerners, did not challenge southern racism. That southern society was to be strictly segregated was never openly questioned by leaders of the campaign. The issue was settled by the first president of the Conference, the venerable old Confederate J. L. M. Curry: "The white people are to be the leaders, to take the initiative, to have the directive control in all matters pertaining to civilization and the highest interest of our beloved land. History demonstrates that the Caucasian will rule."[24] In the age of Social Darwinism, it is doubtful that the northern business leaders in the movement differed much in their racial attitudes. Just a generation removed from Reconstruction and its perceived excesses of the Yankee teachers in the South, northern reformers had to appear particularly sensitive to white southern sensibilities.

The politically astute campaigners argued successfully that the proper kind of education for African-Americans would directly benefit whites. These "southern progressives" proposed a limited, special education for blacks: industrial and agricultural education. The model was already in place as whites were making Booker T. Washington the most powerful African-American of the era. "From Hampton came a Moses, and Tuskegee was born," wrote William H. Baldwin, president of the Southern Railroad and a leader of the campaigns.[25] Baldwin argued unabashedly for maximum use of "the negro [sic] and the mule" to perform the heavy labor to produce economic prosperity in the South.[26] As indicated in chapter one, perhaps nowhere was the economic viewpoint of the movement more powerfully revealed than by Walter Hines Page: "In an ideal economic state, if we were to construct it as ruthlessly as Plato constructed his ideal Republic, we should kill every untrained man; for he is in the way. He is a burden, and he brings down the level of the economic efficiency of the whole community."[27]

Reproduction, Resistance, and "Philanthropy"

The "Captains of Industry" and other business leaders possessed immense power over American society. They were the strongest force in politics as well as in economics in the nation. They could easily have their way with southern education. Through closely allied funds, among them the General Education Board (Rockefeller money), Peabody Fund, John F. Slater Fund, Phelps-Stokes Fund, Julius Rosenwald Fund (Sears and Roebuck), and the Anna T. Jeanes Foundation, industrial education became the curriculum for African-Americans sanctioned by elite white America. The Anna T. Jeanes Foundation was particularly significant in the elementary schools. It sent trained teachers (all African-Americans) to provide demonstration lessons, particularly on industrial, agricultural, and homemaking education, to rural black teachers throughout the South. During the 1915-16 school year, as an example, Jeanes teachers visited 910 of North Carolina's 1,046 African-American schools.[28] Other funds established training schools for older youth. The Slater Fund helped build 355 black training schools with an industrial curriculum and normal courses to train teachers. Tuskegee and the black land-grant colleges established in 1890 also trained large numbers of teachers in the industrial philosophy.

Some African-Americans accepted an industrial curriculum; others resisted. Between 1914 and 1916, Thomas Jesse Jones, a white agent of the Phelps-Stokes Fund, and a team of inspectors conducted a major study of how well black land-grant schools were adhering to the agricultural and industrial curriculum. He was appalled. Industrial schools were being subverted by blacks into academic institutions; curricula officially industrial were literary in practice.[29] Sometimes the resistance was overt. When possible, black teachers drove white supremacist faculty away, even with fist fights in some cases. Under black control, these schools "quickly became teacher-training institutions whose academic emphasis was more literary than industrial and agricultural."[30]

Usually resistance was covert. What Henry Allen Bullock called hidden passages were found to escape the imposed curriculum. African-American teachers did what other American teachers often do in periods when "reforms" are being imposed—subvert the changes by pretending to embrace them, take whatever financial support is being offered, and provide the education that seems to best meet the needs of students.

Without much regard for logical niceties, African-American teachers were often able to merge industrial and academic curricula in everyday practice and to separate desirable goals of industrial and agricultural education from the worst of its racial bias. Following the Jeanes curriculum, African-American teachers encouraged students to garden with tomato clubs for girls and corn clubs for boys, and learning how to build sanitary privies was an important part of the curriculum. But, in addition, when the Jeanes teacher was out of sight, black teachers offered a basic curriculum not much different from the rural white schools down the road. As an example, Virginia Estelle Randolph, a rural black teacher and, later, Jeanes supervisor in Virginia, taught girls homemaking and boys how to make baskets from honeysuckle vines, but she also visited the local white school "to see what the teachers there were doing for their pupils," wanting to be "certain that her pupils were exposed to and given the best."[31]

African-Americans who opposed industrial education had nationally famous as well as local heroes such as Virginia Estelle Randolph. Chief among them was W. E. B. DuBois, graduate of Fisk College and a Harvard Ph.D. He argued that African-Americans should refuse to submit to their degraded position in the caste system and that industrial training should be secondary to a literary and professional education for black leaders. In 1903 in his powerful book, *The Souls of Black Folk*, DuBois challenged directly Washington's policies of submission, gradualism, and compromise in a chapter entitled provocatively, "Of Mr. Booker T. Washington and Others."[32]

DuBois was one of the founders of the National Association for the Advancement of Colored People (NAACP) and was for many years the editor of its journal, *The Crisis*. For decades the NAACP developed legal precedents in a campaign to overturn the case of Plessy *v.* Ferguson. The separate but equal doctrine in the Plessy decision was the constitutional foundation for special, inferior schools for African-Americans.

The NAACP conducted a brilliant legal campaign.[33] In the 1930s and 1940s, lawsuits forced integration in professional and graduate schools. Border states such as Maryland, Arkansas, Missouri, Oklahoma, and Texas, rather than states in the deep South, were chosen because the NAACP attorneys knew that the public outcry from whites would be less intense, and court decisions were more likely to be accepted, however grudgingly. Professional and graduate schools rather than K through 12 or undergraduate schools were chosen, in part because relatively few students would be involved, and those would be adults. The specter of interracial sex is the last refuge of a bigot, and the NAACP leaders knew that one of the rallying cries of racists when public school segregation was finally found unconstitutional would be that schooling children together would lead to intermarriage and "mongrelization" of the races. In these early cases, integrating adults in college towns such as Norman, Oklahoma, or Columbia, Missouri (already hopelessly liberal in the minds of racists), was possible whereas racial integration of elementary or secondary school students would be much more difficult.

Most importantly, cases were easier to win because the "separate but equal" fiction was difficult to sustain when facilities for African-American students didn't exist at all. For example, the University of Missouri had one of America's highest rated journalism schools, but there was no place in Missouri for an African-American to study journalism. Missouri and other states passed legislation providing tuition grants for qualified African-Americans to attend out-of-state professional and graduate schools. However, the courts refused to accept the premise that Missouri could meet the "equal protection of the laws" requirement of the 14th Amendment by paying tuition to out-of-state universities for its black citizens. When, faced with lawsuits forcing integration, Oklahoma and Texas established separate state law schools for African-Americans at Lawton University and Prairie View A & M; the courts found this fiction of "separate but equal" too difficult to support.

These precedents in law were important but insufficient as the basis for changing a policy as fundamental as racial desegregation in elementary and secondary schools. Changes in public attitudes were necessary before the Supreme Court would dare overturn the Plessy decision. The discovery of starving prisoners, gas ovens, mass graves, and other horrors of the holocaust at the end of World War II caused some Americans to recognize, however reluctantly, the consequences of official policies of racism. Cold War rhetoric about the lack of democracy and civil liberties in Communist countries eventually caused many Americans to face their own hypocrisy. President Harry S. Truman courageously desegregated all departments of the federal government, including the armed forces. And federal courts in a series of cases in the 1940s and early 1950s overturned carefully constructed legal barriers that had kept African-Americans from voting.

In the early 1950s, the NAACP attorneys, under the able direction of Thurgood Marshall, brought several public school desegregation cases before the Supreme Court. After intense lobbying by the newly appointed Chief Justice, Earl Warren, on May 17, 1954, a unanimous Court, in Brown *v.* Board of Education of Topeka, found state-mandated racial segregation unconstitutional. Plessy *v.* Ferguson was finally overturned.

If we use the metaphor of "the great detour," the Brown decision did not put black schooling on the same road as white schooling; it only turned African-American education in that direction. The Brown decision came at the time of the "big red scare," and the John Birch Society and other ultra-conservative organizations denounced the Supreme Court as part of a communist conspiracy. "Impeach Earl Warren" signs appeared on billboards across the country almost overnight. Segregationists adopted a policy of "massive resistance," arguing that the Court decision simply could not be enforced against the will of white

Southerners. Prince Edward County, Virginia, closed down its public school system rather than integrate. With the revival of the KKK and the organization of White Citizens Councils, intimidation and violence directed against African-Americans rivaled that of a century before.

Court decisions ordering desegregation were insufficient, and legal dual systems were only dismantled in a great counter campaign that included civil disobedience: the civil rights movement of the 1960s. The courageous civil rights workers in the South were aided by mass media, particularly television. The Cold War mentality of public officials caused them to be concerned with the television images of racial injustice broadcast around the globe: "the massive nonviolent response of black people in the South confronted with an array of cattle prods, clubs, and fire hoses wielded by cursing southern law enforcement units provided dramatic and shocking television viewing . . ."[34]

State-mandated dual school systems were dismantled, but efforts to truly integrate public schools have had only limited success. The Civil Rights Act of 1964 which permitted withholding federal funds from schools that engaged in officially-sanctioned segregation is a powerful weapon against overt discrimination. And the 1971 Supreme Court Case of Swann *v.* Charlotte-Mecklenburg Board of Education allowed wide-spread busing to discourage "white flight" from desegregated schools. But busing was simply too unpopular with whites to be politically feasible as a means of fostering desegregation.

Even when black and white students were in the same building, they often experienced separate and unequal education. Peter Clark's observations about student subcultures at "Hamilton High" in the 1970s are typical of studies of race relations in desegregated high schools. The most noticeable aspect of student life at Hamilton High "was the cleavage between black and white students."[35] In his year as a participant/ observer in the school, Clark saw only a dozen or so black and white students communicating "with each other on a regular basis." Informal interaction between black and white students was simply not a part of the school culture.[36] Even sport was racially segregated. African-Americans dominated in basketball and football, whereas whites played soccer, lacrosse, and tennis.[37]

In desegregated schools, academic expectations for African-American students are often low. At Hamilton High, many teachers "were only too glad to leave the blacks loafing in the halls rather than challenging them in the classroom, and they were negligent in reporting cuts because they did not want disruptive students in their classes."[38]

Disappointment with desegregated schools has caused some African-Americans to look with more than a bit of nostalgia at the segregated schools of the past. Middle-class blacks, particularly, "remember" the all-black academic high schools where demanding black teachers accepted no excuses for failure to learn. Memories of such schools may not reflect objective reality; we all tend to have too rosy pictures of past schools. Part of the backward glance involves a sense of loss, a recognition that integration has had negative as well as positive effects. Obviously, African-Americans don't want to return to the legal status they had in American apartheid, but they may look longingly at the rich community life under black control in an earlier era.[39]

A *Newsweek* story of the 1994 reunion of the former all-black Sadie V. Thompson High School of Natchez, Mississippi, exemplifies this view of the virtues of such schools. The theme of the article was pride–in the school and in graduates: "But those of us who went to Thompson never got the message that we were second rate, unequal, unwanted. Not us. We were bound for glory. And we got there."[40] The expectations of the principal and teachers were high. "We were smart and we were expected to achieve. Even the athletes." Too often black males see getting good grades as acting like a wimp. The alumni at all-black Thompson remembered that "in those days, it wasn't a 'white thing' to get good grades," and males competed as hard as females for academic rewards: "with the classy girls you had to show that you had some brains."[41]

Conclusion

With this historical context it may be easier to see why those committed to equity and justice in education are so impatient with unequal facilities, differentiated curriculums, and academic tracking. Persons dedicated to social justice and who have even a limited understanding of the history of race and education in our society find it difficult to accept rationalizations that unequal facilities are a result of inherited taxing systems impracticable to change, that differentiated curriculums are an unbiased way of preparing youth for their futures, and that academic tracking is simply a method for more effective learning. African-American anger at the racially biased tracking system in Selma, discussed in the introduction to the chapter, was justified by 300 years of experience with education policies aimed at reproducing the racial inequalities existing in the broader society. Teachers ought to be on the side of those resisting racial inequities.

Persons who support (and have struggled for) racial integration and a common curriculum are sometimes disconcerted by a growing number of African-Americans who want community or neighborhood schools, even if the students are all or primarily black, and a different (in some cases an Afrocentric) curriculum. Differences of opinion are, of course, essential to a healthy democratic, pluralistic society, and there is not a consensus among African-Americans any more than among white Americans about educational policies.

Furthermore, the goal of the civil rights movement, including the campaign to dismantle dual school systems, was not to replace an "inferior" black culture with a "superior" white culture but to destroy a caste system that granted power, rights, and privileges to one race while denying them to another. African-American educational philosophers and civil rights activists did not struggle for a literary or classical education because of the intrinsic value of that Eurocentric curriculum, but because it was the only canon that the gatekeepers of the racist society would accept for people attempting to enter academia or the professions. Education for a multicultural world requires both changes in the traditional canon to reflect the pluralistic nature of our culture and the possibilities of persons choosing from among a variety of curriculums.

Notes

1 For an excellent discussion of the issue of historical repression see William F. Pinar, "Curriculum as Social Psychoanalysis: On the Significance of Place," *Curriculum as Social Psychoanalysis: The Significance of Place*, eds. Joe L. Kincheloe and William F. Pinar (Albany: State University of New York Press, 1991).

2 "America in the 21st Century: A Demographic Overview," Population Reference Bureau, Inc., 1989; Sally Reed and R. Craig Sautter, "Children of Poverty: The Status of 12 Million Young Americans," Kappan Special Report, Phi Delta Kappa, (June, 1990).

3 For an updated edition of a well-known history of America's exalted faith in schooling see Henry J. Perkinson, *The Imperfect Panacea: American Faith in Education, 1865-1990* (New York: McGraw-Hill, 1991).

4 Jeannie Oakes, *Keeping Track: How Schools Structure Inequality* (New Haven: Yale University Press, 1985).

5 Joel Spring, *American Education: An Introduction to Social and Political Aspects*, 5th edition (New York: Longman Publishing Group, 1991), pp. 120-21.

6 Bernard Bailyn, *Education in the Forming of American Society* (Chapel Hill: The University of North Carolina Press, 1960), p. 14.

7 Lawrence A. Cremin, *American Education: The Colonial Experience, 1607-1783* (New York: Harper Torchbooks, 1970), p. xiii. Cremin expanded his definition later to include what is learned as well as what is taught.

8 Mrs. George Barnum, "On the Industrial Upbuilding of Southern Cities and Communities," *Proceedings of the Third Capon Springs Conference*, 1900, pp. 60, 61.

9 Charles S. Sydnor, *Slavery in Mississippi* (Baton Rouge: Louisiana State University Press, 1966).

10 Stanley M. Elkins, *Slavery: A Problem in American Institutional and Intellectual Life* (Chicago: the University of Chicago Press, 1963). For a critique of Elkins' thesis, see Herbert G. Gutman, *The Black Family in Slavery and Freedom, 1750-1925* (New York: Vintage Books, 1976).

11 Henry Allen Bullock, *A History of Negro Education in the South* (New York: Praeger Publishers, 1970).

12 James D. Anderson, *The Education of Blacks in the South, 1860-1935* (Chapel Hill: The University of North Carolina Press, 1988), p. 17. If you wish to pursue the topics discussed in this chapter, I recommend Anderson's book.

13 Edgar W. Knight, *Education in the United States*, 3rd edition (Boston: Ginn and Company, 1951), p. 380.

14 Bullock. For detailed accounts of everyday life among African-Americans and their relationship with whites, see Gutman, *The Black Family in Slavery and Freedom.*

15 Thomas L. Webber, *Deep Like the Rivers: Education in the Slave Quarter Community, 1831-1875* (New York: W. W. Norton and Company, Inc., 1978), p. 247.

16 Webber, p. 249.

17 C. Vann Woodward, *The Burden of Southern History* (Baton Rouge: Louisiana State University Press, 1960), p. 13.

18 Clinton B. Allison, "The Appalling World of Edgar Wallace Knight," *Journal of Thought* 18 (Fall 1983).

19 Anderson, p. 7.

20 Jacqueline Jones, *Soldiers of Light and Love: Northern Teachers and Georgia Blacks, 1865-1873* (Chapel Hill: University of North Carolina Press, 1980); Ronald E. Butchart, *Northern Schools, Southern Blacks, and Reconstruction: Freedmen's Education, 1862-1875* (Westport, CT: Greenwood Press, 1980). Because of changes in the treatment of race (and gender), they have replaced a well-known older study: Henry L. Swint, *The Northern Teacher in the South, 1862-1870* (Nashville: Vanderbilt University Press, 1941).

21 C. Vann Woodward, *The Strange Career of Jim Crow* (New York: Oxford University Press, 1955).

22 Merle Curti, "The Black Man's Place: Booker T. Washington, 1856?-1916," *The Social Ideas of American Educators* (Totowa, NJ: Littlefield, Adams and Company, 1971 [1935]); Henry J. Perkinson, "Booker T. Washington," *Two Hundred Years of American Educational Thought* (New York: David McKay Company, 1976). For a discussion of difficulties in interpreting Washington, see Harvey Neufeldt and Clinton Allison, "Education and the Rise of the New South: An Historiographical Essay," *Education and the Rise of the New South, eds.* Ronald K. Goodenow and Arthur O. White (Boston: G. K. Hall and Co., 1981).

23 Curti; Perkinson.

24 J. L. M. Curry, "Education in the Southern States," *Proceedings of the Second Capon Springs Conference* (1898), p. 18.

25 William H. Baldwin, "The Present Problem of Negro Education, Industrial Education," *Proceedings of the Second Capon Springs Conference* (1898), p. 68.

26 Clarence Karier, "American Educational History: A Perspective," paper presented at the Annual Meeting of the Southern History of Education Society (Atlanta, November 12, 1971), p. 102.

27 Walter Hines Page, *Proceedings of the Seventh Conference for Education in the South* (1904), p. 105.

28 *North Carolina Biennial Report of the State Agent of Negro Rural Schools*, 1917.

29 John R. Wennersten, "The Travail of Black Land-Grant Schools in the South, 1890-1917," *Agricultural History* 65 (1991).

30 *Ibid*, p. 54.

31 *The Jeanes Story: A Chapter in the History of American Education, 1908-1968* (Jackson, MS: Southern Education Foundation (1979), p. 25.

32 W. E. B. DuBois, *The Souls of Black Folk* (New York: Signet Classics, 1969 [1903]).

33 Richard Kluger, *Simple Justice* (New York: A. A. Knopf, 1976).

34 Joel Spring, *Deculturalization and the Struggle for Equality: A Brief History of Dominated Cultures in the United States* (New York: McGraw-Hill, 1994), p. 80.

35 Gerald Grant, *The World We Created at Hamilton High* (Cambridge: Harvard University Press, 1988), p. 59.

36 *Ibid.*, p. 59.

37 *Ibid.*, p. 60.

38 *Ibid.*, p. 75.

39 See Henry Louis Gates Jr., *Colored People: A Memoir* (New York: Knopf, 1994).

40 Vern E. Smith, "We Wanted to Be the Best," *Newsweek* 74 (July 18, 1994), p. 53.

41 *Ibid.*, p. 53.

VII

Gender and Education: How Are Gender Biases Reflected in Schools?

Comic pages are a good indicator of what is on Americans' minds. In 1992, "Doonesbury" and "Sally Forth," among others, were depicting the misadventures of girls in schools, particularly their difficulties in getting teachers to pay attention to them. In one strip, Alex, the Doonesbury's daughter, is in tears because the teacher continually ignores her to call on the boys. Her mother says that maybe she should talk with the teacher. Alex responds, "Mom, she'll never call on you! Send Daddy." Popular culture was responding to the American Association of University Women's (AAUW) Report, *How Schools Shortchange Girls*, which was released in February, 1992.[1]

"Consciousness raising" about issues of gender bias in schools was obviously one of the goals of the AAUW Report. Public reaction must have far exceeded the most optimistic expectations of the AAUW. *Time*, *Newsweek*, the wire services, as well as local newspapers gave the Report extensive coverage. Television news and talk shows interviewed the researchers whose findings were featured in the Report. Jane Pauley (spouse of Garry Trudeau, creator of "Doonesbury") had an extended segment on her television program that included interviews with well-known gender equity educational researchers, Myra and David Sadker, whose research was prominently featured in the Report. Popular and "family" magazines responded with feature stories on the Report, including, so help me, an excellent synopsis in *Better Homes and Gardens*.[2] Teachers' journals gave the Report detailed coverage. In my state, *Tennessee Teacher* carried a mutli-page synopsis the month following its national release.[3] The Report received generally favorable responses but was criticized and lampooned in editorials and on radio talk shows by the religious and political right.

The release of the Report coincided with the "National Education Summit on Girls," which was attended by more than thirty national education and youth groups. U. S. Secretary of Education Lamar Alexander and Assistant Secretary Diane S. Ravitch were invited but did not attend. In an interview with *Education Week,* Ravitch, who headed the Department of Education's Office of Educational Research and Improvement, was highly critical of the Report, saying, according to *Education Week,* that gender bias was "not a problem in schools."[4]

Although commonly known as the American Association of University Women Report, *How Schools Shortchange Girls* was a joint publication with the National Education Association. The AAUW contracted with the Wellesley College Center for Research on Women to prepare the Report. The Wellesley Center did not conduct new research but synthesized the existing research on girls in public schools. Most of the research reported in the study was empirical research based on classroom observation and ethnographic studies with trained observers sitting in public school classrooms over extended periods of time, observing and tallying classroom interactions.

According to the Report, girls are invisible in the current national reform documents about public schools. The documents refer to "students," "youth," or "eighth-graders," as if all students were the same, thereby suggesting that the sexes are treated equitably.* According to the Report, nothing could be further from the truth: gender bias is common in teacher-student relations, the curriculum, and in standardized tests.

The issue in "Doonesbury" was easy to lampoon: girls receive significantly less teachers' attention than boys, in part because boys demand it; they are more aggressive. When boys call out answers and comments in class, teachers tolerate or encourage

---

*The authors used sex "when referring to individuals as biologically female or male, and gender when also referring to different sets of expectations and limitations imposed by society on girls and boys," p. 3. Sex is biological; gender is also social.

it. Girls are more often rebuffed and told to raise their hands for recognition. Even when they don't volunteer, teachers call on boys more often. Although numerous research studies find this type of classroom interactions common, teachers usually deny that it is true of their classroom–at least until someone does a tally of their interactions with students. African-American girls try more often than white girls to interact with their teachers, but they have even less success. "Teachers may unconsciously rebuff" black females according to research reviewed for the Report.[5]

Differences in teacher interactions with students are a matter of quality as well as quantity. Teachers encourage boys' intellectual growth by urging and prodding them to find their own answers to problems. Girls who are having difficulties are often simply given the answers. Beginning even in preschool, teachers are more likely to find topics and activities with greater appeal to boys than to girls. Teaching methods based on competition are still common in school even though these methods match the learning styles of boys better than girls. Girls learn better in projects and activities that are based on cooperation rather than competition. These gender biases are deeply rooted in the history of American schooling as we shall see in the historical section of this chapter.

Textbooks and other curriculum materials either ignore females or treat them in stereotypical ways. Even though materials are more inclusive and less sexist than they were a generation ago, bias continues. The Report summarized a 1971 study of the most-used U. S. history textbooks. The study found that no text devoted more than one percent of its space to women, and "women's lives were trivialized, distorted, or omitted altogether."[6] While recognizing improvements, the Report stated that textbooks still contain egregious "examples of omission, tokenism, and gender stereotyping."[7] A major problem in the treatment of gender (and of race and ethnicity as well) is the famous person approach: well-known women are included in text and illustrations, but the story is still told from a male viewpoint, focusing on issues of male interest. Textbooks rarely present the perspective of women or of cultural minorities. An

African-American female is quoted: "In twelve years of school, I never studied anything about myself."[8]

The Report responds forcefully to critics of multicultural education:

> Critics have called Ethnic Studies and Women's Studies "political," as if a curriculum that leaves women out altogether is not also "political." Multicultural work has been termed "divisive" without recognizing that an exclusively white male curriculum is divisive when it ignores the contributions others make to society."[9]

Academic progress for females has been uneven. The gender gap in science has not declined and may even be increasing. Again, teacher behavior may be, in part, responsible. One study found that when teachers needed students to help with science demonstrations, they used boys seventy-nine percent of the time.[10] On the other hand, the Report concluded that gender differences in mathematics achievement are small and declining. However, even girls who are top students in science and mathematics choose careers in those fields "in disproportionately low numbers."[11] The Report was critical of the vocational curriculum for females because it focuses on home economics and other sex-stereotyped courses that lead "to dead-end, low-paying jobs," another issue on which I will provide a historical perspective later in this chapter.[12]

Perhaps the most disturbing part of the Report is the review of the literature on what happens to the self-esteem of girls in school: it goes down year by year. The research indicates that girls learn "helplessness" and to doubt their own abilities. If girls don't do well, they blame it on their lack of ability. If boys do poorly, they say they didn't try hard enough. Males are more likely to drop out of math and science classes because they can't do the work; females drop out because they lack confidence in their ability. The problems of adolescents go well beyond what happens to them in school, of course, but the shattered self-esteem of adolescent females is powerfully revealed in the fact that they attempt suicide four to five times more often than males.[13]

Sexual harassment is often related to young women's loss of a sense of self-esteem. Sexual harassment of girls by boys and sometimes by teachers is increasing in the public schools.* The Report defines sexual harassment as "the unwelcome verbal or physical conduct of a sexual nature imposed" on someone by another person.[14] The someone is usually female; girls are harassed four times as often as boys. Although prohibited by federal law under Title IX of the 1972 Higher Education Act, school authorities often permit or tolerate sexual harassment. Rather than seeing it as "serious misconduct," school officials "too often treat it as a joke."[15] The message, intended or not, from school officials to both sexes is that girls and women are unworthy of respect, and it is appropriate for boys to exercise power over girls. "Boys would treat us with respect," said one young woman in a discussion of what would be an ideal school experience; "if they run by and grab your tits, they would get into trouble."[16] That seems little enough to ask.

The following is among the forty "Recommendations" of the Report:

> State certification standards for teachers and administrators should require course work on gender issues, including new research on women, bias in classroom-interaction patterns, and the ways in which schools can develop and implement gender-fair multicultural curricula.[17]

As a professor of the social foundations of education, my experience over the years in dealing with gender issues has sometimes been difficult. Some education students and teachers, particularly men, have been unwilling to accept the existence of gender biases in schools, even after reviewing many of the research studies that were later synthesized in the Report. Occasionally some students have even been hostile, insisting I was making problems where none actually existed. The wide dissemination of the Report has made such discussions easier; the existence of many of these gender biases is now common knowledge in American culture.

---

*The AAUW also commissioned *Hostile Hallways: The AAUW Survey on Sexual Harassment in America's Schools,* June 1993.

Historical Perspectives

The AAUW Report instructs us on how much more needs to be done. Although progress has been made in American history, the education gender gap has been only slowly and painfully reduced. In colonial America, beliefs about a separate and inferior place for women in society made even literacy problematic for girls. In the first generations of Europeans in America, children of both sexes received much of their education at home, and boys were much more likely to be taught to read. In addition, some parents sent their young children to a woman in the community, often a widow or poorer "goodwife," who kept the children and taught them what she had the time or inclination to teach, including the alphabet. Both girls and boys attended these dame schools. Of contemporary institutions, dame schools served many of the same purposes of child care centers and kindergartens. Their primary function was often baby-sitting, a place to put children while their parents worked, keeping them "out of fire and water."[18]

As discussed in chapter one, town schools (often called reading and writing schools) were established in Massachusetts in 1647 by the Old Deluder Satan Act. They became common throughout New England. Although the law did not specify that only boys could attend, a consensus was quickly established that they were for boys only, and there are few references to girls attending these public schools for several generations. They were part of the male sphere. Parents sometimes resisted the bias against schooling for their daughters. In *Learning Together*, their excellent history of coeducation in American schools, David Tyack and Elisabeth Hansot title the first chapter: "Smuggling in the Girls: Colonial New England." In this chapter they discuss the practice of parents "smuggling" their daughters into the public schools by paying teachers extra to teach girls before or after the regular all-boy school session.[19] Wealthier parents often sent their daughters to private (venture) schools.

Historian Kathryn Kish Sklar finds diminishing gender inequities in schooling between 1750 and 1820.[20] Town schools were admitting more girls, giving them access to basic literacy.

At first, girls were allowed to attend only summer schools when the older boys and male teachers were working in the fields, leaving only girls and boys too young to farm free to attend school. Summer schools gave teaching opportunities to women and helped create the female teaching corps discussed in chapter three. With this precedent, towns and school districts increasingly accepted (or were forced to accept) the responsibility of providing schooling for girls. By the 1790s, New England districts were fined for not funding female schooling. Historian Linda Kerber writes of the ambivalence with which these developments in schooling for girls were regarded: "They could be welcomed with excitement. They were also met with profound distrust."[21]

In addition to the anti-female biases of the time, some members of the elite had economic motives for limiting girls' schooling. For example, Levi Shepard of Northampton, Massachusetts, was a strong opponent to female education. He was also, coincidentally, an important manufacturer of duck cloth for ships' sails and often hired to work in his factory poor children who did not attend school.[22] And, of course, the whole social order would be threatened with servant girls neglecting their work and writing "love letters instead."[23]

The more prestigious Latin Grammar schools, also established by the Old Deluder Satan Act, were exclusively male institutions in the beginning. The law establishing such schools in New Haven, Connecticut, copied the Old Deluder Satan Act almost verbatim. But to make sure there was no possible misunderstanding the meaning of the word "youth" in the law, the trustees of the school clarified its meaning in 1684: "all Girles be excluded as Improper and inconsistent with such in Grammar Schoole."[24] Changes came (often excruciatingly) slowly in schooling for girls, but a century later, in grammar schools (which increasingly taught English as well as Latin) girls were attending in larger numbers.

Schooling opportunities made a noticeable change in women's literacy during the late colonial period. The quarter-century after 1760 was the period in which women developed the skills that "allowed them to compose coherent sentences."[25] "Benjamin Franklin received occasional hesitant and almost illiterate notes from his wife Deborah and his friend Margaret Stevenson," Kerber notes, but fluent letters from Sarah, Deborah's and his daughter, and from Polly, Margaret Stevenson's daughter. The younger generation had the benefit of improved schooling for women.[26] By the census of 1850, adult, white New Englanders of both sexes were almost all classified as literate, a revolutionary change for American women. Such change could only take place because women demanded and worked for it. "One is struck by the hunger of some women for learning," Kerber writes, "for access not only to skills but to wisdom, and by their expression of resentment at their exclusion from the world of books."[27]

Social change was difficult for generations of men who were emotionally attached "to the traditional image of women as passive, inferior, and subordinate members of society."[28] You can feel the longing of John W. Wayland in 1825 when he remembers an earlier time: "Ladies of that day never followed any profession, or meddled with men's affairs–they could teach small children their alphabet and work samplers."[29] Although the changing images of women threatened the patriarchal social order, part of the problem was simply the male ego. Men were frightened that their shortcomings might be noticed and corrected by women; how awful to think that "wives and daughters would look over the shoulders of their husbands and fathers and offer to correct" their spelling errors.[30]

A leading nineteenth-century magazine for privileged women, *Godey's Lady's Book,* warned young females who wanted an education that men need to think they are superior to women and that it behooved women to look up to men and to be modest about their own intellectual attainments. At the same time, *Godey's* assured men that educated women would be happier in their private lives but would not compete with them for public honors.[31] School textbooks, until the middle of the nineteenth century, warned children that educated women were often unattractive to men. On the other hand, pioneer women educator Zilpah Grant observed that it was difficult for an educated woman to find a man worthy of her deference.[32]

American school textbooks in the nineteenth century both reflected and affected common beliefs about gender. Ruth

Elson, a historian of the social ideas of school textbooks, writes that ideas about sexual equality in economics, politics, or society are not to be found in the textbooks. Although treatment of women in other cultures is criticized ("Pagans treat women as domestic animals"), in America, school textbooks tell children that men and women are already equal and improvement is unnecessary.[33] In these textbooks, women do not have their own interests or ambitions; they spend their lives "in happy submission to the will of others."[34] Before marriage a female is completely subjected to the will of her father, regardless of how terrible he may treat her. Cruelty "by no means releases me from my duty to him; had he a thousand errors, he is still my father."[35] After marriage, complete obedience is, of course, owed to her husband. These textbooks advise children, both boys and girls, that a wife should recognize that "the end of thy being is to soothe him [the husband] with tenderness and to recompense his care with soft endearments."[36] The most popular textbook of the early nineteenth century, Noah Webster's spelling-book, depicts an ideal married couple:

> Art thou a husband? Treat thy wife with tenderness; reprove her faults with gentleness.
>
> Art thou a wife? Respect thy husband; oppose him not unreasonably, but yield thy will to his, and thou shall be blest with peace and concord; study to make him respectable; hide his faults.[37]

Elson concludes that nineteenth-century children who believed their textbooks "would assume that women were a breed apart, happy in servility, important for instinct rather than for intelligence."[38]

Beliefs about women's proper (i.e., subservient) place in society were in large part a legacy of traditional Christian theology. But, in American social history, Christianity has often been both a conservative and a radical force, and an evangelical revival in the new nation, the Second Great Awakening, was one of the forces that encouraged schooling for women. Partly it was a new impetus for an older Protestant belief that all, including women, were responsible for studying the *Bible* to assure their own salvation. Partly it was an expression of patriotic fervor in the new republic that American Protestant women had higher status and more responsibility than in decadent (and Catholic) Europe where women were portrayed "as beasts of burden or as playthings of the aristocracy, not partners with men in creating republican virtue, as in America."[39] Many of the leaders in women's education were also activists in the religious awakening, and they often saw a special responsibility for educated women: to act as moral guardians over men who were naturally inclined towards immorality, even perversion.[40]

Historian Linda Kerber has used the term Republican mother to characterize a cluster of ideas about the important role of learned women in educating their children. These ideas or attitudes were a major justification for schooling women following the Revolutionary War. Women needed to be educated, so the argument went, in order to prepare their sons and future sons to better serve their nation. Women could not govern or even vote, but they could play a major role in producing a moral and just society by training their sons in civic virtues. In a society that placed great faith in education, to claim that educated women could influence their sons to govern a democracy wisely was a persuasive argument. Pioneers of women's education such as Mary Lyon, Catharine Beecher, and Emma Willard seized on the idea: educated women would be better companions for their husbands and wise teachers of their children.[41] In addition, educated women could further their beneficial influence beyond their own immediate family by becoming teachers which has added the metaphor of "the teaching daughters" to the Republican mothers.[42]

The ideology of the Republican mother was successful; opponents of schooling for girls were silenced. Even the *Southern Literary Messenger*, no bastion of liberal thought on women (or anything else) argued in 1835 for the "cultivation of the female intellect," calling it "absolutely necessary for the happiness, and for the well-being of those whom providence may render dependent upon her guidance, her councils, or her affections." The *Messenger* further suggested that an educated woman would be a companion, "and not the plaything of the other sex."[43]

But notice that the arguments for women's education were not based on notions of gender equality. The sexes were to be kept in their separate spheres—culturally, economically and politically. Women, Horace Mann argued, should be protected from the "muck and corruption" of politics "just as they should be barred from joining the military or practicing the law."[44] And girls in schools would not be encouraged to enter the male sphere but would be bolstered in their own. The curriculum was the textbook and textbooks made it clear that boys and girls had separate lives. Girls were told not to engage in boys' activities. A little girl is prohibited from helping her brother build a cart because it is not "a proper employment for a young lady." A girl falls from a swing; the moral is made explicit: "A swing is not a safe thing for a little girl."[45] Girls are taught that they are "guardians of purity" and much is made in the textbooks about their role in modeling moral behavior. One textbook writer, however, got a bit carried away with his homonyms in this pre-Freudian practice sentence: "A snake chased the chaste girl."[46] The proper roles for the sexes were, according to the conventional wisdom, fixed by nature. As the 1823 *Analytical Spelling Book* put it:

> Pinks smell sweet.
> Good girls are neat.
> A leech sucks blood.
> Ducks play in mud.[47]

The Female Seminary Movement

Women educators used the image of the republican mother, later expanded to an ideology that historians sometimes call domestic feminism, to justify more advanced liberal arts education for females than could be offered in public elementary schools. These educational pioneers such as Emma Willard, Catharine Beecher, and Mary Lyon created female seminaries which stressed academic purposes as well as moral development. These private schools were named academies, institutes, or seminaries, ambiguous terms that were sometimes used interchangeably—the term seminary didn't have the strict connotation of training religious workers in the nineteenth century that it has today. Female schools were somewhat more likely to be named seminaries and male schools, academies. The most prestigious of the schools, Willard's Troy Female Seminary (1821), Beecher's Hartford Female Seminary (1832), Lyon's Mount Holyoke (1836), and a growing number of others established before 1850 proved that women students were able to master any curriculum offered to males; indeed, they were often more intellectually rigorous than men's colleges of the period.

The females attending these schools were often quite young, in part because of the need to maintain enrollments. Troy took students as young as twelve and Hartford, fourteen.[48] Pre-teens were admitted to seminaries throughout the country. A group of men examining the quality of learning at the Elizabeth Female Academy in Mississippi in 1829 were "delighted" and "astonished" at the academic quality of the students: "Certainly it is a matter of astonishment to witness little girls of 12 years of age treat the most abstruse problems of Euclid as mere playthings."[49]

Enrollments in female seminaries increased as more girls attended public elementary schools. The seminaries were a major source of trained teachers before normal schools became widespread. The alumna of these seminaries often saw teaching as a missionary field, and they left the Northeast by the hundreds to bring literacy and Christ to the South and to the West. They so often married the local clergymen with whom they labored in the missionary field that the female seminaries were sometimes referred to as Adam's rib factories (did you pass this test of Biblical literacy?).

These teachers sometimes established their own female seminaries, spreading the idea across the nation, including the South where planter families increasingly wanted to educate their daughters at home rather than send them to the North with its growing abolitionist sentiments. Historian Anne Firor Scott has analyzed the influence of Emma Willard in spreading the "Troy idea" across the country. Scott estimates that eventually there were 200 schools modeled after Troy Female Seminary. Willard stayed in touch with her graduates who were establishing these schools, continually watching over and encouraging them—an early example of networks that have been so important in feminists' movements.[50]

Traditionally the curriculum of the elite in America (and in the rest of the western world) was the classical languages, particularly Latin which distanced gentlemen not only from lower classes but "from their mothers and sisters" as well.[51] The female seminaries were determined to prove that women could learn any subject that men could, but they were also concerned with a more utilitarian, but not a less academic, curriculum. The best known of the seminaries offered mathematics; modern languages; the sciences including chemistry, physics, botany, and geology; as well as Latin and sometimes Greek. Usually, classical studies continued to be more important in the male academies and colleges, but they were losing a long battle for their central place in the curriculum. Classical studies became increasingly under attack because, in utilitarian America, they were not practical and, in the evangelical fervor of the Second Great Awakening, they were pagan studies. Increasing numbers of educators would agree with one of their southern brethren who cried out against having the young study the "squabbling of heathen gods and goddesses" when they were "ignorant of the character and attributes of the true God."[52]

Westerners, in particular, tended to want a more "practical" education. In the 1830s, Solon Robinson of Indiana endorsed the separate, lower sphere for women at the same time he campaigned for schools that were:

> . . . Useful. Not a piano, French, Spanish or flower daub education, but one that will make the men scientific farmers and mechanics, and intelligent public officers and *acting* legislators, and the women fit to become honored and husband-honoring wives of such citizens. . . .[53]

Often, however, leaders of western academies claimed a more utilitarian curriculum than was actually offered. It was a way to give lip service to the practical bias of the frontier West, a way to disarm the advocates of a traditional, classical curriculum. And what is "utilitarian" is contextual; studies may be practical only if one is fixed in a particular sphere. In frontier Missouri, for example, schools for "young ladies" often emphasized "feminine subjects" such as ornamental needlework including the making of "counterpanes, ladies dresses, caps, handkerchiefs, toilets, and samplers of the latest fashions."[54]

And some of the seminaries were practical with a vengeance. The Moravian Seminary for Young Ladies at Hope, Indiana, in the 1870s had a domestic economy curriculum with the objective "that our Daughters may be as Corner Stones, Polished after the Similitudes of a Palace." Catharine Beecher's *Domestic Economy* was the textbook. Some of the topics treated were:

Difficulties peculiar to American women
Remedies for the preceding difficulties
Healthful food
Healthful drinks
Early rising
Preservation of good temper in a housekeeper
Care of domestics
Care of infants
Washing, starching, and ironing
Whitening, cleaning, and dyeing.[55]

Some of you may have noticed that when a male feels threatened by a bright, well-informed woman he often responds with a "put down" in the form of a joke. A continuing theme in American educational history has been bad jokes about educated women. Graduates of the female academies and seminaries were often awarded degrees, but different ones from men college graduates. M.P.L. (Mistress of Polite Literature), as an example, was common. But even these degrees that recognized the separate spheres for women were sometimes ridiculed by the mean-spirited humor of males who were opposed to formal schooling for women. In 1835, the Springfield, Massachusetts, newspaper commented on an academy that had just awarded some M.P.L. degrees: we recommend "M.P.M. (Mistress of Pudding Making,) M.D.N. (Mistress of the Darning Needle,) M.S.B. (Mistress of the Scrubbing Brush,) and especially M.C.S. (Mistress of Common Sense). . . . And we furthermore recommend to them to procure some well-qualified Professors, from among the farmers' wives . . . to teach the young ladies the useful art of house-wifery."[56]

Historians differ on how much these seminaries helped women liberate themselves from their limited sphere. Certainly, much of the curriculum, formal and hidden, aimed to reproduce the traditional gender roles (at Oberlin "some men were allowed to bake bread, all women had to darn their male classmates' socks").[57] Keith Melder has called these seminaries "masks of oppression," arguing that they accepted "oppressive definitions of woman's sphere."[58] Their intellectual offerings were as good as the best men's colleges, but rather than trying to liberate women from their patriarchal society, they supported all of the conventional social inequalities of the day. The atmosphere was authoritarian with the women's lives being circumscribed by petty rules: "They will not expose themselves at windows & front doors." By "expose," the teachers meant permitting their faces to be seen from outside."[59]

Barbara Miller Solomon, in *In the Company of Educated Women*, agrees that the leaders of these seminaries "would not have declared themselves feminists."[60] She also agrees that they accepted rather than questioned prevailing ideas of what women should be, including "precepts of piety, purity, obedience, and domesticity."[61] But, she concludes, they also pushed the margins of what men would allow, and they recognized that they were only at the beginning place of a long, arduous struggle. Academic learning was powerful; it gave women intellectual tools with which to resist their oppression.

Coeducation in School: Separate Spheres in Life

Tyack and Hansot consider coeducation to be arguably the most important development in the gender history of our public schools. Surprisingly, teaching boys and girls together was not a major controversy and was not even a deliberate and conscious policy decision in most school districts. Coeducation (mixed schools was the prevalent term through much of the nineteenth century) was so commonplace to Americans that it was considered part of the natural order of things, although foreign visitors often found it "strange and disturbing."[62] Adolescents of both sexes studying in the same classroom was considered particularly bizarre.

Coeducation was practical. Most Americans lived in rural areas in the nineteenth century, and there were not enough children to support separate schools for boys and girls, if schools were to be within walking distance. Of course the rural South later supported separate schools for blacks and whites, but the profound prejudices against race mixing were quite different from feelings about gender mixing. And coeducation was common even in the conservative South: "The fact that males and females had separate spheres did not mean that they needed to be physically separated in school, anymore than in family or church."[63]

It is important to notice that even though most people supported coeducation, they were also committed to separate spheres for women and men. They failed to recognize that girls and boys learning together was a threat to a patriarchal society, particularly when girls often did better than boys academically.

As the excerpts from the nineteenth-century textbooks that you read earlier suggest, children were to prepare to live in separate spheres in their adult lives, but there was a great deal of equity inside the district one-room schools: "Boys and girls were expected to follow the same rules, to learn the same subjects, and to be judged by similar standards."[64] Outside the formal lessons they would perform gender-specific chores; boys would keep the fire going and girls would clean the classroom. But most of the time they were treated much the same.

A study of John Wirt Dinsmore's 1908 manual for teachers, *Teaching A District School: A Book for Young Teachers*, confirms the conclusion that coeducation was so pervasive that it was taken for granted, but, that it did not, at the same time, challenge the separate spheres for the sexes. Dinsmore was dean of the Normal Department of Berea College, and his textbook was widely used by rural teachers. Teacher education students sometimes claim that they receive too much theory and not enough practical advice in their teacher education program. Dinsmore's book was devoid of anything but practical advice. It was a 246 day-by-day manual of detailed instructions for every day and for every occasion.[65]

Coeducation was not mentioned in the book; it was simply taken for granted. Gender for the most part was invisible; and boys and girls were lumped together as pupils or children, as the AAUW Report suggests they continue to be. Occasionally a comment reveals a matter-of-fact acceptance of separate spheres. Dinsmore instructs the teacher in getting the school-house ready for a new year: "The girls can do their part by washing the windows, cleaning the walls and scrubbing the floor. A boy should black the stove."[66]

Dinsmore's curriculum material was often carefully gender balanced. An example can be seen in these arithmetic problems: "If John has one apple, and his mother gives him one more, he will have two apples" is followed by "If Mary has three pennies and spends one for candy, she will have two pennies left."[67] Occasionally, although the subject matter lesson is the same, separate spheres outside of school are matter-of-factly recognized. Penalties for bad grammar were high for either sex, but the separate spheres were clearly recognized. In one exercise, an army private lost his chance to be an officer when he said, "I seen him yesterday, but I haven't saw him to-day." A "young lady" applying for a teaching position lost her chance for the job when she replied to a question, "No, I haven't saw any of them."[68]

There are sometimes strong hints in Dinsmore's advice to teachers that boys are more privileged than girls. His suggestions about what to do on a dull afternoon when "energy is at a low ebb" was to learn a new song. "Get some boy who is skillful with the mouth organ to play an accompaniment, and have all the school march around the room."[69] The bias is particularly strong in his suggestions for a "Field Day." He advises the teacher to "give every boy a chance to take part and to choose the particular sport in which he excels."[70] He indicates that field days can "be a powerful incentive to keep the larger boys in school."[71] He does not mention girls in his discussion of field days.

Acceptance of separate spheres was most powerfully revealed in Dinsmore's extended discussion of teaching about occupations, lessons that he thought particularly important. This is the only place in the book where there are separate sections for males and females. Discussions of professions are limited to boys: "If any young man desires to be a minister of the gospel, he needs the very best education that can be secured."[72] Females are mentioned only in the discussion of teaching as a "profession." "No ambitious young man or woman of scholarly tastes," he advises, "need hesitate to choose the profession for a life work."[73]

In his section on "Occupations for Women," he admonishes teachers that girls "are not expected to choose trades or professions for life. Every moral girl should look forward to homemaking and be fitted for domestic duties." He endorses schools that teach domestic arts, particularly cooking and sewing, skills that every woman should be proud to possess, and which don't "hinder her from presiding with grace at the piano, or from being an ornament in society."[74] However, he warns the teacher that some women will have to support themselves. They may not be "born teachers" and need to be informed about other occupations. The only ones Dinsmore mentions, however, are "clerks, bookkeepers, stenographers." "But aside from a few glittering attractions," he warns, "to follow any of these is to lead a hard life. To sit at a desk or typewriter many hours a day and work at high speed; to do the same thing over and over again in the same way is monotonous and tiresome."[75] Obviously, Dinsmore thinks it is better for women to marry.

The AAUW Report indicates that boys and girls are disciplined differently, and that boys are usually disciplined more severely. This difference seems to have existed throughout history. In the nineteenth century, boys were more often described as greater discipline problems than girls. John Wayland, remembering his coeducation school in 1825, wrote that "Girls were very seldom punished; if ever, very slightly; boys were frequently whipped or kept in after school."[76] The punishment of sitting in the girls' section indicates that sometimes there was physical separation, but it did not seem to be common. Geraldine Clifford who studied hundreds "of first hand accounts of schools" finds that students were rarely physically separated by sex; "separation was impracticable, and many Americans were just not that fussy about details."[77]

There were often complaints that local districts even failed to provide separate privies for boys and girls. A particular concern was that girls shouldn't have to read the boys' graffiti. But many rural dwellers of the time were lucky to have one outhouse and that seemed quite enough for a school. "In the mid-1880s in

Illinois," as an example, "1,740 schools had only one privy, and 1,180 had none."[78]

Tyack and Hansot present a benign picture of gender equity in nineteenth-century rural schools. They see the experiences of boys and girls as quite similar, and they correctly warn that "Looking only for differences in the treatment of girls and boys can obscure similarities."[79] Still, as I reflect on the unconscious nature of most of the gender bias in the 1992 AAUW Report, it is difficult not to suspect that in the nineteenth century when the gender spheres were much more pervasive, unequal treatment must not have been at least as great as now. Even in the nineteenth century, coeducation caused educators to question whether teaching methods that were good for males were necessarily good for females. As an example, a major debate began in the 1820s about the value and suitability of competition, or emulation as it was called then. Women teachers of girls were particularly critical of this common practice, exemplified by the omnipresent spelling bee.[80] The 1992 AAUW criticism of the practice indicates that tradition won the nineteenth-century debate.

According to both the conventional pedagogical wisdom of the nineteenth century and recollections of school days, coeducational schools resulted in respectful, refined, and restrained relations between the sexes rather than sexual harassment. Advocates of coeducation argued it is a mistake to attempt to keep boys and girls "pure" by keeping them apart: "monks, as a class, are more passionate and corrupt than merchants . . . imagination of the absent sex in the separate schools is worse than its presence in the mixed."[81] The *Pennsylvania School Journal* in 1854 reported on a study that found that boys in all-male schools "will habitually engage in improprieties if not vices of which they would not dare to be guilty in other circumstances." The *Journal* allowed that the same was true of all-female schools but "not to the same extent."[82]

John Swett, the "Horace Mann of California," argued that teaching boys and girls together would result in boys learning to regard women's character as "pure and holy" and girls learning to "respect manliness and manhood." He presented an idyllic, nostalgic picture of his own school days in rural New Hampshire:

> My pleasantest memories of school-days are associated with the bright-eyed little girls who came to school in summer mornings, bringing May flowers and lilacs in their hands. Nobody ever told any of the boys of our school that it was a sin to love them. [These] farmers' girls, red-cheeked, barefoot too, and dressed in homespun, taught us our first lessons of faith in the purity and nobleness of womanhood.[83]

Small, rural schools with children from families who knew each other well undoubtedly curbed sexual harassment. Coeducation advocates liked family metaphors: brothers and sisters learning together, and respecting and protecting each other. But these innocent portrayals of sexual relationships between boys and girls in school may have had more to do with Victorian modesty about public recognition of sexual matters (and a traditional blindness in American culture about the sexual activity of children) than with the treatment of girls by boys. It is always best not to confuse idyllic pictures of the past with their reality.

Women in High Schools

Urban high schools which were becoming more common after mid-nineteenth century were the focal point of much of the challenge to coeducation. Conservative clergy and educators were afraid that coeducation might lead to "foolish flirting and frivolity," if not worse, among hormone-saturated adolescents. The objections to coeducation often sprang from a class bias. Increasingly cities were populated by immigrants: poor, often dirty, and, in the eyes of privileged Anglo-Americans, peculiar if not bizarre. Delicate daughters had to be protected from contamination by rude, vulgar, and obscene immigrant and low-class boys.[84]

Another major attack was based on the argument that coeducation presented a grave threat to the health of young women. The best-known and most effective critic of coeducation was a prominent Boston physician and sometime instructor of medicine at Harvard, Edward Clarke. In 1873 he published a popular book, *Sex in Education*, that went through a number of editions. He maintained that during puberty blood should not go the brain but to the developing reproductive organs. "Monstrous brains and puny bodies . . . flowing thought and constipated bowels" would result from adolescent girls competing intellectually with boys.[85] Revealing the sexist attitudes of the day, another physician cautioned against intellectual activity by young women: "Why should we spoil a good mother by making her an ordinary grammarian?"[86] These attacks on the practice of coeducation were ultimately unsuccessful.

The beginning of this century is often portrayed by educational historians as the golden age of gender equality in American high schools. Despite the earlier debate, high schools at the turn of the century were almost all coeducational. The number of girls in high school was too small to justify single-sex schools, and school administrators supported coeducation in theory and in practice. Women studied the same curriculum as males and made better grades. Of course subtle differences in the treatment of males and females, such as that described in the AAUW Report, is difficult for historians to capture and probably often went unrecognized by the participants at the time.

Few school administrators, teachers, or students expected or wished the high school to alter the separate sphere of men and women, although some feminists of the period hoped that coeducation would eventually help in the struggle for women's emancipation. High schools were still elite institutions at the end of the nineteenth century; in 1890 less that five percent of secondary-school-age students were enrolled. The school population was upper-middle class, Protestant, and English speaking. Most of the female students were not in high school to enhance their employment opportunities, although high school would certainly help if a middle-class young woman had to earn a living in clerical work or in retail sales. Historian John Rury concludes that most young women who enrolled did so because they enjoyed high school. It was a good place to socialize with friends and parents were comfortable that their daughters would not be in close contact with the "wrong types" as experience made clear that immigrants, Catholics, and "coarse" and vulgar lower-class youths were simply not in high schools.[87]

The Boy Problem

The change from a similar to a differentiated curriculum for young women and men was in part a result of girls doing too well in high school. The boy problem was that girls were more successful in high school than the boys were. Obviously, according to male educators and psychologists, something is wrong with high schools if girls do better than boys. According to these critics, the problem was that coeducation schools were too masculine for girls, and more serious, they were "too sissy for boys."[88]

G. Stanley Hall, one of the best known educational psychologists of the time and "the champion of masculinity in education," worried that sexual distinctions were being lost and that the schools should push to "their uttermost" to "make boys more manly and girls more womanly."[89] He addressed the annual meeting of the National Education Association in 1903, warning them that the high school had been feminized in almost all regards and was becoming an increasingly bad place for boys.[90]

And boys were dropping out at a higher rate than girls. By 1900 there were twice as many females as males in high school, over 60 percent of high school graduates were females, and college enrollments were growing faster for women than for men. A 1900 observation about high schools may remind some of you of your teacher education classes. An educator in *School Review* wrote that it "is not an infrequent experience to find a good-sized class with not a single boy, while a class with twenty girls and two or three stray and lonesome boys is fairly common."[91] The fault of course was women teachers who were "feminizing the boys" and female students who were "shaming the boys by outperforming them" in a "feminized" curriculum.[92]

Another part of the problem was that the boys were often discipline problems in an institution that didn't meet their needs. Lower-class boys often resisted by forming countercultures to make the teachers' lives miserable; "in a sex-education lecture on the 'evils of self abuse,' one boy defied the teacher by masturbating in the back of the classroom."[93] (One of my former students observed a similar incident by an American

Indian student in a class that was in cultural rebellion against a teacher.)

Many educators saw an answer to the boy problem in a gender-differentiated curriculum with emphasis on vocational education. Working-class boys, particularly, they argued could be persuaded not to drop out if school prepared them for a decent job as an adult. Another solution was interscholastic athletics which helped keep working-class boys in schools and aided in reversing "the image of high schools as a feminine domain."[94]

The Girl Question

In addition to "the boy problem" as a cause of differentiation in high school experiences, there was what Jane Bernard Powers has called "the girl question."[95] The context for "the girl question" was a widespread (and for many Americans alarming) perception that women's roles were changing, especially following W.W.I and the emergence of the flappers of the 1920s. The women's sphere was enlarging, and many seemed to be escaping from it entirely. For over a century the limits of women's roles had been fairly much set by the idea of domestic feminism: women could extend their natural responsibilities as wives and mothers into jobs as teachers or nurses or into behind-the-scenes advocates of playgrounds, parks, and improved schools as examples. But in the twentieth century they were breaking loose, taking jobs of all kinds, deciding not to marry, divorcing their husbands, agitating for and receiving the right to vote, and dominating enrollments in secondary schools and going to college in ever-increasing numbers.[96]

These changes were often perceived by conservatives as a social breakdown, perhaps abetted by too much of the wrong kind of education for women. Then and now conservatives looked to the traditional family as the "means by which morality and order could be restored to American life in the twentieth century."[97] The "girl question" was what kind of education is appropriate for the legitimate roles that women should play in society.

The powerful "social efficiency" movement in education, a precursor to the education for life adjustment movement discussed in chapter five, was in ascendancy in the early decades of this century. Among other things, social efficiency educators contended that all people should be scientifically selected and trained for the particular roles they would play as adults. Educators and policy makers used the assumptions of social efficiency to develop an education to prepare women for their "preferred" adult roles as wives, mothers, and homemakers. According to a 1930 survey of the National Council of Education, men and women should be prepared for very different family responsibilities: "The man to provide the income; to be in the home when practicable and help in training the children. The woman to buy wisely; to manage the home so as to preserve the family morale; to preserve her own health and bear children intelligently; to train the children wisely."[98] David Snedden, a leader in the social efficiency movement, suggested changes in the high school curriculum to prepare women for their roles as homemakers, including "applied" courses in chemistry and physics designed specifically for women's use at home.[99]

Since homemaking was "women's true profession," advocates of homemaking education became a powerful force in lobbying for curricular changes in secondary schools. Powers called the homemaking education lobby "an organized effort to feminize women's education in the United States."[100] The equivalent of industrial education for boys, it would help girls "avoid the unnatural craving for careers."[101] Its advocates presented homemaking education as a panacea for all kinds of social ills:

> Men would be lured from saloons by good food cheerfully cooked in efficient kitchens; farm women would stay in the country and farm conditions would improve generally; middle class women's lives would take on new meaning through scientific homemaking and municipal housekeeping. Working class women would manage their husbands' pay checks better; immigrants would be Americanized; domestic service employees would perform more efficiently; race efficiency would improve; infant mortality would be reduced, and the quality of life for Americans in general would be substantially improved.[102]

The following document exemplifies the knowledge of homemaking that could be gained from the social efficiency movement. Christine Frederick instructs how to peel potatoes efficiently:

1. Walk to shelf adjacent to sink and get pot.
2. Walk to storage, carrying pot, and fill it with potatoes.
3. Return from storage, laying pot directly on vegetable preparing surface near sink.
4. Pick up knife (from nail above this surface).
5. Pare potatoes directly into pail (soiling no surface).
6. Wash potatoes and fill pot with water.
7. Wash and hang up knife (on nail above sink).
8. Walk with pot and lay on stove.[103]

Home economics education is another example of attempts (however unconscious) to use schools to reproduce the inequities that exist in the broader society. Women were to be trained to play their traditional roles in society, and poor and minority women were to stay at the bottom of the labor market by being trained in domestic skills. Home economics education (and industrial education generally) was class biased. Social efficiency educators accepted the class divisions of society and trained working-class children for menial jobs as if their place in the economic hierarchy was fixed.[104] In 1928, social efficiency advocate Snedden proposed "that girls of less than median intelligence will probably be rearing two-thirds of the children of 1940-1970 and thus the bulk of all money put into home economics should be used to serve . . . girls of this type."[105] Poor and minority young women were provided a watered down curriculum of special academic courses and "practical domestic science." For minority women particularly, home economics education was a travesty. Spanish-speaking women in the Southwest were released from their jobs as maids to be instructed "in housekeeping, cleaning, cooking, and food service."[106] Home economics was more often compulsory for black women than for white women, and black women were sometimes encouraged by school officials to take special training for domestic services.[107]

Resistance to attempts by schools to reproduce societal inequities is a major theme of this book. And young women (and their parents) resisted attempts by educators to train them for poor-paying, menial jobs. Only when home economics education was compulsory did girls enroll in it in large numbers.

Usually they were able to escape. For the school year 1927-28, as an example, only 16.5 percent of female high school students enrolled in home economics. As George Counts observed at the time: "The girls who were supposed to rejoice at the opportunity of being equipped for the responsibilities of the home and motherhood have been interested in other things."[108]

Commercial education to train office workers was much more popular with students and their families. Office clerks, typists, and, especially, secretaries were considered middle-class occupations and the job opportunities were great. In 1870 there were less than 1,000 women working in offices, by 1910 the number had risen to 100,000 and by 1920 to 1,000,000.[109] Whereas home economics was "openly ideological" and aimed at supporting family values and traditional gender roles, commercial education was "market driven," and young women enrolled because they wished to prepare for what they perceived as desirable jobs.[110]

The office as a workplace was much more desirable than the factory, cleaner, less exhausting, more interesting, and usually better paying.[111] Most women still expected to eventually play traditional roles by marrying, and offices were considered good places to find a suitable husband. A young woman in the 1920s ponders her future: "I want to get married some time. If I'm a teacher I'll never meet any men and so what is there to do except be a stenographer." Her friends, she says, are "all stenographers who hoped to become executive secretaries and marry the boss, or failing in this, to some lesser male members of the office force."[112]

"The boy problem" and "the girl question" led to less gender equality and greater differentiation of the curriculum in American high schools. In the first thirty years of the twentieth century, female enrollment in academic courses dropped precipitously, particularly in mathematics and physics. And the special courses for homemakers mentioned above caused even the same subject to be taught differently for males and females. The superintendent of schools in Marinette, Wisconsin, explained how chemistry, as an example, was different: for girls it was "largely around the chemistry of the home, of cooking, food values, and adulteration in their detection, while that of the boys' classes is like that of physics, more technical and 'scientific,' calculated to be of most service to them in higher institutions and in the arts and crafts."[113] Extracurricular activities were also increasingly gender specific with males serving as president of the student body and females as secretary.[114] And of course school athletics, dominated by boys, became increasingly more important in the life of schools.

Historians differ somewhat on the final result of these attempts at gender curriculum differentiation. John Rury writes of the "appearance of a distinctive *female* curriculum in American high schools" after a tradition of equality of half a century;[115] whereas Tyack and Hansot conclude that in the academic courses, "the vast majority of boys and girls studied the same curriculum in the same room under the same teacher."[116]

Conclusion

Teachers are usually not consciously and deliberately sexist any more than most are deliberately racist. Their sexism, like their racism, is generally unconscious and unrecognized. That is why the raising of consciousness by feminists is important. Kathleen Weiler makes the point that after the achievements of the feminists early in this century, including the right to vote, "the language of feminism" was not so often heard and the discriminatory practices described in the historical account that you have just read went unchallenged for the most part. Educators did not recognize the biased nature of their practices. The silences of feminist voices led "eventually to the deeply sexist and discriminatory culture of the 1950s."[117]

A powerful and articulate women's movement of the 1960s and 1970s again raised the consciousness of educators and policy makers about the sexual bias that existed in public schools. The language of feminism again challanged gender inequities and sexist practices that had simply been taken for granted for generations.

Growing public awareness and the surprising political power of the women's movement led to the passage of Title IX of the Higher Education Act of 1972 requiring sexual equality in education programs at all levels. The Carter administration used

Title IX effectively in the 1970s to end blatant gender discrimination. Unfortunately, during the conservative restoration of the 1980s, the national administrations were ideologically opposed to pursuing gender equity. Officials hostile to feminism, often from the religious right, in the Education and Justice Departments refused to use (and attempted to abrogate) the powers that they possessed under Title IX. Indeed in the 1980s, politically powerful voices were again being heard about the intellectual ability of women. In 1989, as an example, Pat Robertson, leader of the right-wing Christian Coalition, said that "the key in terms of mental (ability) is chess. . . . There's never been a woman Grand Master chess player. Once you get me one, then I'll buy some of the feminism . . ." (Actually, there were already two women Grand Masters at that time. Since then three more have been added, including fifteen-year-old Judit Polger, the youngest Grand Master in history.)[118]

The major importance of the AAUW Report is that it once again raises the consciousness of American teachers, policy makers, and parents. It is also important for teachers to notice that feminists don't all speak with one voice. Early generations of feminists struggled for equal access, equal curriculums, and equal financial support. The Report, for the most part, does not argue for gender neutrality, but for strategies and curriculums that honor differences in the ways males and females know and learn.[119]

Notes

1 *The AAUW Report, How Schools Shortchange Girls: A Study of Major Findings on Girls and Education*, The AAUW Educational Foundation, 1992.

2 Michael Walker, "Gender Bias: Is Your Daughter's School Prepping Her for Failure," *Better Homes and Gardens* (April 1993), p. 71.

3 "How Schools Shortchange Girls: The AAUW Report," *Tennessee Teacher* (March 1992), p. 59.

4 Millicent Lawton, "National Groups Promise Steps to Combat Inequities for Girls," *Education Week* (February 19, 1992), p. 5.

5 *The AAUW Report*, p. 70.

6 *Ibid.*, p. 62.

7 *Ibid.*, p. 60.

8 *Ibid.*, p. 61.

9 *Ibid.*, p. 67.

10 *Ibid.*, p. 72.

11 *Ibid.*, p. 27.

12 *Ibid.*, p. 42.

13 *Ibid.*, p. 79.

14 *Ibid.*, p. 73.

15 *Ibid.*

16 *Ibid.*, p. 82.

17 *Ibid.*, p. 85.

18 David Tyack and Elisabeth Hansot, *Learning Together: A History of Coeducation in American Public Schools* (New York: Russell Sage Foundation, 1992), p. 19.

19 *Ibid.*, p. 14.

20 Kathryn Kish Sklar, "The Schooling of Girls and Changing Community Values in Massachusetts Towns, 1750-1820," *History of Education Quarterly* 33 (Winter 1993).

21 Linda K. Kerber, "Nothing Useless or Absurd or Fantastical: The Education of Women in the Early Republic," *Educating Men and Women Together: Coeducation in a Changing World*, ed. Carol Lasser, (Urbana and Chicago: University of Illinois Press, 1987).

22 Sklar, p. 521.

23 Tyack and Hansot, p. 26.

24 James Axtell, *The School Upon a Hill: Education and Society in Colonial New England* (W. W. Norton & Company, Inc., 1976), p. 176.

25 Sklar, p. 514. See also Mary Beth Norton, *Liberty's Daughters: The Revolutionary Experience of American Women, 1750-1800* (Boston, 1980).

26 Kerber, p. 40.

27 *Ibid.*, p. 44.

28 Glenda Riley, "Origins of the Argument for Improved Female Education," *History of Education Quarterly*, 9 (Winter 1969), p. 456.

29 "Comments are Made on A Co-Educational School in Harrisonburg, Virginia, 1825," *A Documentary History of Education in the South Before 1860, Vol.* 5, ed. Edgar W. Knight (Chapel Hill: The University of North Carolina Press, 1953), p. 390.

30 Tyack and Hansot, p. 26.

31 Riley, p. 463.

32 Barbara Miller Solomon, *In the Company of Educated Women: A History of Women and Higher Education in America* (New Haven: Yale University Press, 1985), p. 26.

33 Ruth Elson, *Guardians of Tradition: American Schoolbooks of the Nineteenth Century* (Lincoln: University of Nebraska Press, 1964), pp. 301-303.

34 *Ibid.*, p. 303.

35 *Ibid.*

36 *Ibid.*, p. 307.

37 Clifton Johnson, *Old-Time Schools and School-books* (New York: Dover Publications, Inc., 1963 [1904]), p. 178.

38 Elson, p. 312.

39 Tyack and Hansot, p. 28.

40 Kerber; Solomon; Tyack and Hansot, pp. 36-38.

41 Kerber. Also see Linda K. Kerber, *Women of the Republic: Intellect and Ideology in Revolutionary America* (Chapel Hill: University of North Carolina Press, 1980) and Norton, *Liberty's Daughters.*

42 Joan M. Jenson, "Nor Only Ours But Others: The Quaker Teaching Daughters of the Mid-Atlantic, 1790-1850," *History of Education Quarterly*, 24 (Spring 1984).

43 *Southern Literary Messenger*, Vol. I (May, 1835), quoted in Knight, p. 402.

44 Tyack and Hansot, p. 35.

45 Elson, p. 304.

46 *Ibid.*

47 Johnson, p. 211.

48 Solomon, p. 22.

49 "A Report of the Examination at Elizabeth Female Academy in Mississippi is Made, 1829," Knight, p. 398.

50 Anne Firor Scott, "The Ever Widening Circle: The Diffusion of Feminist Values from the Troy Female Seminary, 1822-1872," *History of Education Quarterly*, 19 (Spring 1979), p. 12.

51 Kerber, p. 38.

52 Quoted in Solomon, p. 23.

53 Solon Robinson, "Where Did He Get His Education, " Albany *Cultivator* (September, 1838), reprinted in *Solon Robinson: Pioneer and Agriculturalist*, Herbert Andrew Kellar, (ed.) *Indiana Historical Collections*, 21 (1936), p. 93.

54 Margaret McMillan and Monia Cook Morris, "Educational Opportunities in Early Missouri," Part II, *Missouri Historical Review*, 33 (July, 1939), p. 478.

55 Paul E. Belting, "The Development of the Free High School in Illinois," *Journal of the Illinois State Historical Society*, 11 (October, 1918) p. 331.

56 *Republican and Journal*, Springfield, Massachusetts, March 14, 1835, quoted in Knight, p. 404.

57 Solomon, p. 24.

58 Keith Melder, "Mask of Oppression: The Female Seminary Movement in the United States *Proceeding of the New York State Historical Association*, 72 (1974), p. 262.

59 *Ibid.*, p. 269.

60 Solomon, p. 26.

61 *Ibid.*, p. 25.

62 Tyack and Hansot, p. 1.

63 *Ibid.*, p. 48.

64 *Ibid.*, p. 72.

65 John Wirt Dinsmore, *Teaching A District School: A Book for Young Teachers* (New York: American Book Company, 1908).

66 *Ibid.*, p. 21.

67 *Ibid.*, p. 49.

68 *Ibid.*, p. 152.

69 *Ibid.*, p. 120.

70 *Ibid.*, p. 123.

71 *Ibid.*, p. 124.

72 *Ibid.*, p. 197.

73 *Ibid.*, p. 202.

74 *Ibid.*, p. 207.

75 *Ibid.*, p. 208.

76 Quoted in Knight, p. 390.

77 Quoted in Tyack and Hansot, p. 69.

78 *Ibid.*, p. 70.

79 Tyack and Hansot, p. 72.

80 Nancy Green, "Female Education and School Competition: 1820-1850," *History of Education Quarterly*, 18 (Summer 1978).

81 Thomas Woody, *A History of Women's Education in the United States*, p. 265 (New York: The Science Press, 1929).

82 Quoted in Woody, p. 265.

83 Quoted in Tyack and Hansot, p. 74.

84 John L. Rury, *Education and Women's Work* (Albany: State University of New York Press, 1991), p. 28; Tyack and Hansot, pp. 92-95.

85 Rury, p. 25; Tyack and Hansot, p. 151.

86 Tyack and Hansot, p. 88.

87 Rury, pp. 58, 75, and 86.

88 Tyack and Hansot, pp. 14 and 166.

89 Rury, p. 23.

90 Rury, p. 158.

91 Tyack and Hansot, p. 174.

92 *Ibid.*, p. 155.

93 *Ibid.*, p. 178.

94 *Ibid.*, p. 198.

95 Jane Bernard Powers, *The "Girl Question" in Education: Vocational Education for Young Women in the Progressive Era* (Bristol, PA: The Falmer Press, 1992).

96 *Ibid.*, p. 12.

97 Rury, p. 140.

98 Quoted in Tyack and Hansot, p. 183.

99 Rury, p. 158.

100 Powers, p. 12.

101 *Ibid.*, p. 15.

102 *Ibid.*, p. 22.

103 C. Frederick, *Household Engineering: Scientific Management in the Home* (Chicago: American School of Home Economics, 1915), quoted in Powers, p. 15.

104 Powers, p. 83.

105 Quoted in Powers, p. 87.

106 Powers, p. 88.

107 *Ibid.*, pp. 83-90.

108 *Ibid.*, p. 95.

109 *Ibid.*, pp. 39-40.

110 Tyack and Hansot, p. 215.

111 Powers. p. 118.

112 *Ibid.*, p. 119.

113 Rury, p. 157.

114 Tyack and Hansot, p. 229.

115 Rury, p. 173.

116 Tyack and Hansot, p. 234.

117 Kathleen Weiler, "Women and Rural School Reform: California, 1900-1940," *History of Education Quarterly*, 34 (Spring 1994).

118 From a story in "The Washington Spectator," *The Knoxville News-Sentinel*, Sunday, Jan. 16, 1994.

119 Joan C. Williams, "Deconstructing Gender," *Feminist Jurisprudence: The Difference Debate*, ed. Leslie Friedman Goldstein (Rowman & Littlefield Publishers, Inc., 1992); Glorianne M. Leck, "Examining Gender as a Foundation within Foundational Studies," *Teachers College Record*, 91 (Spring 1990).

Selected Bibliography

The AAUW Report. *How Schools Shortchange Girls: A Study of Major Findings on Girls and Education.* The AAUW Educational Foundation, 1992.

A Nation at Risk: The Imperative for Educational Reform. The National Commission on Excellence in Education, 1983.

A Nation Prepared: Teachers for the 21st Century. The Report of the Task Force on Teaching as a Profession. Carnegie Forum on Education and the Economy, 1986.

Allison, Clinton B. "Students Under Suspicion: Do Students Misbehave More Than They Used To," in *13 Questions: Reframing Education's Conversation,* eds. Joe L. Kincheloe and Shirley R. Steinberg. New York: Peter Lang, 1992.

——. "The Feminization of Teaching Revisited: The Case of the Ne're-Do-Well Man Teacher," in *The Socio-Cultural Foundations of Education and the Evolution of Education Policies in the United States,* ed. James J. Van Patten. Lewiston, New York: The Edwin Mellon Press, 1991.

——. "The Conference for Education in the South: An Exercise in *Noblesse Oblige."* *Journal of Thought* 16 (Summer 1981).

Anderson, James D. The *Education of Blacks in the South, 1860-1935.* Chapel Hill: The University of North Carolina Press, 1988.

Axtell, James. *The School Upon a Hill: Education and Society in Colonial New England.* New York: W. W. Norton and Company, 1974.

Bailyn, Bernard. *Education in the Forming of American Society*. Chapel Hill: The University of North Carolina Press, 1960.

Brumberg, Stephan E. *Going to America Going to School: The Jewish Immigrant Public School Encounter in Turn-of-the-Century New York City*. New York: Praeger Publishers, 1986.

Bullock, Henry Allen. A *History of Negro Education in the South*. New York: Praeger Publishers, 1970.

Butchart, Ronald E. *Northern Schools, Southern Blacks, and Reconstruction: Freedmen's Education, 1862-1875*. Westport, CT: Greenwood Press, 1980.

Callahan, Raymond E. *Education and the Cult of Efficiency*. Chicago: The University of Chicago Press, 1962.

Carper, James G. and Hunt, Thomas C., eds. *Religious Schooling in America*. Birmingham, AL: Religious Education Press, 1984.

Coleman, James S. *Equality of Educational Opportunity*. Office of Education: Washington DC, 1966.

Counts, George Sylvester. The *Selective Character of American Secondary Education*. Chicago: The University of Chicago, 1922.

——. *The Social Composition of Boards of Education: A Study in the Social Control of Public Education*. Chicago: University of Chicago Press, 1927.

Cremin, Lawrence A. *American Education: The Colonial Experience, 1607-1783*. New York: Harper Torchbooks, 1970.

——. *Popular Education and its Discontents*. New York: Harper and Row, 1989.

——. *The Transformation of the School: Progressivism in American Education, 1876-1957*. New York: Alfred A. Knopf, 1961.

Cuban, Larry. *Teachers and Machines: The Classroom Use of Technology Since 1920*. New York: Teachers College Press, 1986.

Curti, Merle. *The Social Ideas of American Educators*. Totowa, NJ: Littlefield, Adams and Co., 1959 [1935].

DuBois, W. E. B. *The Souls of Black Folk*. New York: Signet Classics, 1969 [1903].

Elsbree, Willard S. *The American Teacher: Evolution of a Profession in a Democracy*. New York: American Book Company, 1939.

Elson, Ruth Miller. *Guardians of Tradition: American Schoolbooks of the Nineteenth Century*. Lincoln: University of Nebraska Press, 1964.

Ford, Paul Leicester, ed. *The New England Primer: A History of its Origin and Development*. New York: Teachers College, Columbia University, 1962 [1897].

Ginger, Ray. *Age of Excess*. New York: The Macmillan Co., 1965.

Goldman, Eric F. *Rendezvous With Destiny: A History of Modern American Reform*. New York: Alfred A. Knopf, Publisher, 1952.

Goodlad, John I. *A Place Called School: Prospects for the Future*. New York: McGraw-Hill, 1984.

Grant, Gerald. *The World We Created at Hamilton High*. Cambridge: Harvard University Press, 1988.

Gutman, Herbert G. *The Black Family in Slavery and Freedom, 1750-1925*. New York: Vintage Books, 1976.

Hawes, Joseph M. and Hiner, N. Ray, eds. *American Childhood: A Research Guide and Historical Handbook*. Westport, CT: Greenwood Press, 1985.

——. *Children in Urban Society: Juvenile Delinquency in Nineteenth-Century America*. New York: Oxford University Press, 1971.

Hoffman, Nancy. *Woman's True Profession: Voices from the History of Teaching*. Old Westbury, New York: The Feminist Press, 1981.

Hogan, David John. *Class and Reform: School and Society in Chicago, 1880-1930*. Philadelphia: University of Pennsylvania Press, 1985.

Hollingshead, A. B. *Elmtown's Youth: The Impact of Social Classes on Adolescents*. New York: Science Editions, 1967 [1949].

The Jeanes Story: A Chapter in the History of American Education, 1908-1968. Jackson, MS: Southern Education Foundation, 1979.

Jencks, Christopher, et al., *Inequality*. New York: Basic Books, 1972.

Johnson, Clifton. *Old-Time Schools and School-books*. New York: Dover Publications, Inc., 1962 [1904].

Jones, Jacqueline. *Soldiers of Light and Love: Northern Teachers and Georgia Blacks, 1865-1873*. Chapel Hill: University of North Carolina Press, 1980.

Kaestle, Carl F., ed. *Joseph Lancaster and the Monitorial School Movement: A Documentary History*, Classics in Education, No. 47. New York: Teachers College Press, 1973.

——. *Literacy in the United States: Readers and Reading Since 1880*. New Haven: Yale University Press, 1991.

——. *Pillars of the Republic: Common Schools and American Society, 1780-1860*. New York: Hill and Wang, 1983.

Katz, Michael B. *Alternative Proposals for American Education: The Nineteenth Century*. New York: Praeger Publishers, 1971.

——. *Class, Bureaucracy and Schools: The Illusion of Educational Change in America*. New York: Praeger Publishers, 1975.

——. "The Orgins of Public Education: A Reassessment." *History of Education Quarterly* 16 (Winter, 1976).

Kerber, Linda K. "Nothing Useless or Absurd or Fantastical: The Education of Women in the Early Republic," in *Educating Men and Women Together: Coeducation in a Changing World*, ed. Carol Lasser. Urbana and Chicago: University of Illinois Press, 1987.

——. *Women of the Republic: Intellect and Ideology in Revolutionary America*. Chapel Hill: University of North Carolina Press, 1980.

Kliebard, Herbert M. *The Struggle for the American Curriculum, 1893-1958*. New York: Routledge, 1986.

Kluger, Richard. *Simple Justice*. New York: A. A. Knopf, 1976.

Kozol, Jonathan. *Savage Inequalities: Children in America's Schools*. New York: Crown Publishers, 1991.

Lazerson, Marvin. *Orgins of the Urban School: Public Education in Massachusetts, 1870-1915*. Cambridge, MA: Harvard University Press, 1971.

Leck, Glorianne M. "Examining Gender as a Foundation within Foundational Studies." *Teachers College Record* 91 (Spring 1990).

Lortie, Dan C. *Schoolteacher: A Sociological Study*. Chicago: The University of Chicago Press, 1975.

McCarty, Donald and Ramsey, Charles. *The School Managers: Power and Conflict in American Public Education*. Westport, CT: Greenwood Press, 1971.

Melder, Keith. "Mask of Oppression: The Female Seminary Movement in the United States." *Proceeding of the New York State Historical Association* 72 (1974).

Morison, Samuel Eliot. *The Puritan Pronaos: Studies in the Intellectual Life of New England in the Seventeenth Century*. New York: New York University Press, 1936.

Nasaw, David. *Schooled to Order: A Social History of Public Schooling in the United States*. New York: Oxford University Press, 1979.

Norton, Mary Beth. *Liberty's Daughters: The Revolutionary Experience of American Women, 1750-1800*. Boston: Little, Brown, 1980.

Oakes, Jeannie. *Keeping Track: How Schools Structure Inequality*. New Haven: Yale University Press, 1985.

Perkinson, Henry J. *The Imperfect Panacea: American Faith in Education, 1865-1990*. New York: McGraw-Hill, Inc., 1991.

Peshkin, Alan. *God's Choice: The Total World of a Fundamentalist Christian School*. Chicago: University of Chicago Press, 1986.

Pinar, William F. "Curriculum as Social Psychoanalysis: On the Significance of Place," in *Curriculum as Social Psychoanalysis: The Significance of Place*, eds. Joe L. Kincheloe and William F. Pinar. Albany: State University of New York Press, 1991.

Powers, Jane Bernard. *The "Girl Question" in Education: Vocational Education for Young Women in the Progressive Era*. Bristol, PA: The Falmer Press, 1992.

Preston, Jo Anne. "Female Aspiration and Male Ideology: Schoolteaching in Nineteenth-Century New England," in *Current Issues in Women's History*, Arina Angerman et al. London: Routledge, 1989.

Reed, Sally and Sautter, R. Craig. "Children of Poverty: The Status of 12 Million Young Americans." Kappan Special Report, Phi Delta Kappa (June, 1990).

Reese, William J. *Power and the Promise of School Reform: Grassroots Movements During the Progressive Era*. Boston: Routledge & Kegan Paul, 1986.

Riley, Glenda. "Origins of the Argument for Improved Female Education." *History of Education Quarterly* 9 (Winter 1969).

Rury, John L. *Education and Women's Work*. Albany: State University of New York Press, 1991.

Scott, Anne Firor. "The Ever Widening Circle: The Diffusion of Feminist Values from the Troy Female Seminary, 1822-1872." *History of Education Quarterly* 19 (Spring 1979).

Shor, Ira. *Culture Wars: School and Society in the Conservative Restoration, 1969-1984*. New York: Routledge & Kegan Paul, 1986.

Sizer, Theodore. *Horace's Compromise: The Dilemma of the American High School*. Boston: Houghton Mifflin, 1984.

Sklar, Kathryn Kish. "The Schooling of Girls and Changing Community Values in Massachusetts Towns, 1750-1820." *History of Education Quarterly* 33 (Winter 1993).

Solomon, Barbara Miller. *In the Company of Educated Women: A History of Women and Higher Education in America*. New Haven: Yale University Press, 1985.

Spencer, Dee Ann. "The Personal Lives of Women Teachers: An Intergenerational View." *Teacher Education Quarterly* 14 (Spring 1987).

Spring, Joel. *The Sorting Machine: National Educational Policy Since 1945*. New York: David McKay Co., 1976.

Tyack, David and Hansot, Elisabeth. *Learning Together: A History of Coeducation in American Public Schools*. New York: Russell Sage Foundation, 1992.

—— and Hansot, Elisabeth. *Managers of Virtue: Public School Leadership in America, 1820-1980*. New York: Basic Books, 1982.

——. Lowe, Robert and Hansot, Elisabeth. *Public Schools in Hard Times: The Great Depression and Recent Years*. Cambridge, MA: Harvard University Press, 1984.

——. *The One Best System: A History of American Urban Education*. Cambridge: Harvard University Press, 1974.

——. "Ways of Seeing: An Essay on the History of Compulsory Schooling." *Harvard Educational Review* 46 (August, 1976).

—— and Strober, Myra H. "Women and Men in the Schools: A History of the Sexual Structuring of Educational Employment." Washington: National Institute of Education, 1981. Grant Number NIE-G-79-0020.

Urban, Wayne J. *Why Teachers Organized*. Detroit: Wayne State University Press, 1982.

Warner, W. Lloyd. *American Life: Dream and Reality*. Chicago: University of Chicago Press, 1953.

—— and Associates, *Democracy in Jonesville*. New York: Harper and Bros., 1949.

Warren, Donald, ed. *American Teachers: Histories of a Profession at Work*. New York: Macmillan Publishing Co., 1989.

Webber, Thomas L. *Deep Like the Rivers: Education in the Slave Quarter Community, 1831-1875*. New York: W. W. Norton and Company, Inc., 1978.

Weiler, Kathleen. "Women and Rural School Reform: California, 1900-1940. *History of Education Quarterly* 34 (Spring 1994).

Weis, Lois. "Inequality: A Sociological Perspective in Teacher Education." *Educational Foundations* 1 (Fall 1986).

Wennersten, John R. "The Travail of Black Land-Grant Schools in the South, 1890-1917." *Agricultural History* 65 (1991).

Williams, Joan C. "Deconstructing Gender," in *Feminist Jurisprudence: The Difference Debate*, ed. Leslie Friedman Goldstein. Savage, MD: Rowman & Littlefield Publishers, Inc., 1992.

Woodward, C. Vann. *The Burden of Southern History*. Baton Rouge: Louisiana State University Press, 1960.

——. *The Strange Career of Jim Crow*. New York: Oxford University Press, 1955.

Index